Under Armour Case Analysis

TABLE OF CONTENTS

- Who will implement strategy?
- How will the strategy achieve organization wide commitment?
- Are structuring mechanism properly aligned?
- Are functional area conflicts reconciled to strategy requirements?
- Does leadership inspire commitment to strategy?
- Do reward systems reinforce appropriate behavior?
- Are functional issues addressed and resolved in implementation?
- Is the strategy communicated properly?

I. DIAGNOSIS AND OVERVIEW

Business Description (Under Armour, 2014)

We, Under Armour, Inc. together with our subsidiaries, develop, market, and distribute branded performance apparel, footwear, and accessories for men, women, and youth worldwide primarily in North America, Europe, the Middle East, Africa, the Asia-Pacific, and Latin America. Our brand's moisture-wicking fabrications are engineered in many different designs and styles for wear in nearly every climate to provide a performance alternative to traditional products. We provide various footwear products, including football, baseball, lacrosse, softball and soccer cleats, slides, performance training, running, basketball, and outdoor footwear. We also offer accessories, which include headwear, bags, and gloves; digital fitness platform licenses and subscriptions, as well as digital advertising; and license our brands. We primarily produce our products under the UA Logo, UNDER ARMOUR, UA, ARMOUR, HEATGEAR, COLDGEAR, ALLSEASONGEAR, PROTECT THIS HOUSE, and I WILL trademarks, as well as ARMOURBITE, ARMOURSTORM, ARMOUR FLEECE, and ARMOUR BRA. We sell our products through wholesale channels, including national and regional sporting goods chains, independent and specialty retailers, department store chains, institutional athletic departments, and leagues and teams, as well as independent distributors; and directly to consumers through a network of brand and factory house stores, and Website. Under Armour, Inc. was founded in 1996 and is headquartered in Baltimore, Maryland.

Current Situation (Under Armour, 2014)

In 2013, three drivers pushed the mission forward, and continue to position Under Armour for growth in the future: continued innovation, global expansion, and the acquisition of MapMyFitness. Our customers expect newness and innovative ideas from us and we rose to the challenge in 2013. We enhanced and expanded our platforms to continue to grow with our athletes as their preferences move into new categories and end uses for our products. The strong, continued growth in our core North American business gave us the firepower to continue building the infrastructure and foundation for international expansion. In 2014, we are positioned to tell our story in an authentic and relevant way to consumers around the world, as we reach more athletes than ever before. The next big story we're pioneering is what we call "Connected Fitness," which we took another major step towards growing with our acquisition of MapMyFitness. This puts us in a great position to design open, digital products for the athlete of tomorrow and provide solutions that will help people across the world lead healthier lives. Connected Fitness is growing rapidly and we are positioning Under Armour to be the leader in this space.

Innovation is about creating new platform technologies like Charged Cotton®, or our latest, Cold-Gear® Infrared – none of which existed prior to 2011. It's also about reinventing and improving the performance of our legacy platforms like HeatGear®. Brands are built on trust. Our approach to incorporate innovation into new and existing products is how we continue to build brand equity and trust with our consumer. As we continue to innovate in Footwear, our products help gain market share in football and baseball, and we completely changed how kids dressed on field. Our latest innovation in running – UA SpeedForm™ – leverages our DNA in apparel to deliver what consumers have come to expect from our brand: innovation around fit.

In 2013 we successfully got out our message and helped drive sales by telling our story in a new way to complement our new products through special events participation and holiday marketing tactics. Leveraging our ever increasing brand recognition, in 2013 we continued to expand and invest in partnerships that make Under Armour visible, again helping to drive a strong year for our business. We became the official supplier for the U.S. women's and men's gymnastics teams, and we recently extended our partnership with the U.S. speed skating team. We partnered with the NFL and GE to form Head Health Challenge II. Most recently, we announced game-changing partnerships with the University of Notre Dame and the U.S. Naval Academy. These partnerships not only enhance our connection with consumers, but strengthen our long-standing relationships with key sporting-goods partners. This is the foundation of our North American business and will continue to be a focus in 2014.

Our Direct-to-Consumer channel represented 30% of our business in 2013 and is another way we tell our story, dictate trends, and teach the athlete how to dress head-to-toe. This includes our network of 117 Factory House® Outlet Stores that provide a profitable way to manage our excess inventory and serve as a vehicle to attract more athletes to our brand. We opened two new-concept Brand House stores in 2013, offering a premium shopping experience with an emphasis on specialization and localization. Brand Houses are the intersection of innovation, cutting-edge products, and impactful storytelling. Lastly, we understand how important E-Commerce is to our target market and will continue deploying the right level of assets to ensure we maximize this important and growing channel, while connecting authentically with our athletes.

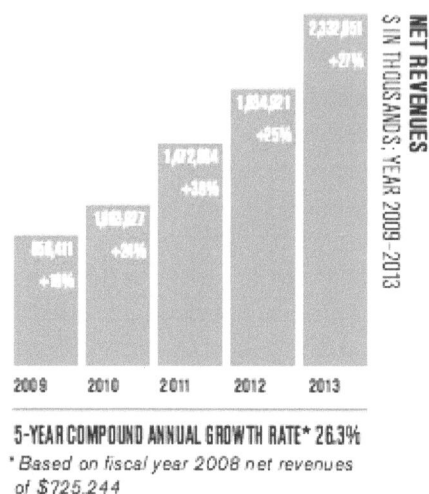

NET REVENUES $ IN THOUSANDS: YEAR 2009-2013

2,332,051 +27%
1,834,921 +25%
1,472,684 +38%
1,063,927 +24%
856,411 +18%

2009 2010 2011 2012 2013

5-YEAR COMPOUND ANNUAL GROWTH RATE* 26.3%
*Based on fiscal year 2008 net revenues of $725,244

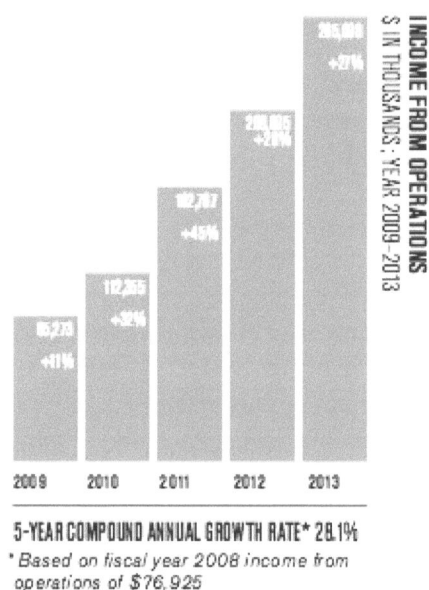

INCOME FROM OPERATIONS $ IN THOUSANDS: YEAR 2009-2013

265,000 +27%
208,685 +26%
162,767 +45%
112,355 +32%
85,278 +11%

2009 2010 2011 2012 2013

5-YEAR COMPOUND ANNUAL GROWTH RATE* 28.1%
*Based on fiscal year 2008 income from operations of $76,925

Our strong growth and cash creation in our North American businesses will help drive and support our global ambition. In 2013, we continued to invest in our team, product, distribution, and marketing efforts throughout the world. For the first time, Under Armour has more offices outside the United States than inside; we are getting our product out to new consumers in new markets. In Europe, we believe we are on the tipping point of success as we increased our focus on developing deeper in-market presence in key countries while also building brand awareness through great partnerships like Tottenham Hotspur. In Latin America, the foundation has been formed for an exciting 2014. We recently began selling our products directly in Mexico rather than through a distributor, and we are now launching our brand in Brazil and Chile. We also announced new partnerships with the football teams Colo-Colo in Chile and Cruz Azul in Mexico, as we lay the foundation for growth outside of the United States in the world's biggest sport. We are committed to being a global brand with global stories to tell, and we are on the way. MapMyFitness will also play a role in our global strategy as it is a leading Connected Fitness platforms with over 22 million registered users around the world as of March 2014, including over 30% located outside of the U.S. We are dedicated to lead in the Connected Fitness space and deliver game-changing solutions that affect how athletes train, perform, and live.

A. Mission, Vision, & Values (Under Armour, 2016)

Mission
Make all the athletes better through passion, design, and the relentless pursuit of innovation.

Vision
Empower athletes everywhere.

Values
- Founding Core Values
    - Innovation
    - Inspiration
    - Reliability
    - Integrity
- 4 Pillars of Greatness
    - Make great product.
    - Tell a great story.
    - Provide great service.
    - Build a great team.

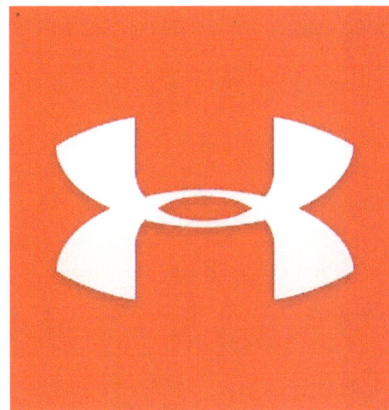

Wills
- Act like a global citizen.
- Think like an entrepreneur.
- Create like an innovator.
- Perform like a teammate.

B. Objectives

For 2013, Under Armour has laid out the following objectives for the company:
- Short-term, double our business ($4 billion in revenues) by 2016; long-term, reach $7.5billion in revenue by 2018
    - Double the amount of infrastructure (with a focus on offices outside of North America) in order to accommodate the growth
    - Increase brand loyalty and customer satisfaction by maintaining and acquiring new partnerships/licenses with organizations to build relationships, strengthen connections, and increase visibility of brand
    - Build brand equity and trust with customer by constantly innovating new and existing quality products
- By 2015, increase foreign market sales to at least 10% of total revenues
    - Focus on infrastructure being built outside North America
    - Focusing on partnering with international manufacturers and distributors and building own Under Armour Stores abroad
- Decreasing excess inventory by increasing inventory turnover by at least 3% (from 143.21 days to under 139 days) by 2015.

⸋ Increase gross profits by 60% (from $1.13 billion to $1.81) by 2016.

C. <u>Corporate Strategy</u>

As part of business strategy, Under Armour focuses on building sponsorship agreements with leading athletes. Currently, our plans are concentrated over product development efforts comprising design, fit and product use. Our core marketing and promotion strategy concentrates on selling its products to high-performing athletes and teams on the high school, collegiate and professional levels. We also focus on meeting consumer demand while improving inventory efficiency over the long term. Under Armour intends to enhance inventory management by focusing on retail merchandising, strategic liquidation through our own retail outlet stores, and forecasting and maximizing the flexibility of supply chain.

D. Policies
The following section on policy has been taken from Under Armour (2014 & 2016).

Diversity
Under Armour's (2016) Code of Conduct outlines equal employment opportunity, harassment, workplace safety, and social relationships as it relates to diversity under the section "Work Environment." Please refer to the next section for more information on diversity.

Ethical Standards/Code of Conduct
Under Armour Inc.'s Code of Conduct in 2016 highlights the following categories:
- **Resources for asking questions**
  - **How to report:** If there is a situation that may violate the code, policies or law, one can report it to the highest level of management on the team, the Human Resources Business Partner for you can report it to the highest level of management on your team, the Human Resources Business Partner for your area or any senior leader in the Human Resources organization, or anyone on the Global Ethics and Compliance team (globalcompliance@underarmour.com). You can also phone the 24/7 hotline (listed below) or log onto Convercent.com/report to report any concern and anonymously if you wish. Information provided through the hotline and Global Ethical and Compliance team is directed to the United States and reasonable effort is made to secure personal data collected to avoid unauthorized use or disclosure such.
  - **Non-retaliation:** No retaliation will be taken against any teammate for raising an ethical concern, question or complaint in good faith. Should that teammate's identity be known, the Global Ethics & Compliance team will monitor any disciplinary action against the teammate to determine if it is retaliatory.
  - **Investigations process:** All legitimate concerns, questions and complaints will. Be taken seriously and handled promptly and professionally with confidentiality maintained to the greatest extent possible. More information can be viewed in Under Armour's Whistleblower Policy on Our House.
- **Work Environment**
  - **Equal employment opportunity:** At Under Armour, we're one race; the Human Race. We are committed to providing equal employment opportunities to all qualified individuals without regard to race, color, religion, sex, pregnancy (including childbirth, lactation, and related medical conditions), national origin, age, physical and mental

disability, marital status family or caregiver responsibilities, sexual orientation, gender identity, gender expression, genetic information (including characteristics and testing), military/veteran status, or any other characteristic protected by local, state or federal law.

- ☐ **Harassment:** Under Armour is committed to a safe, congenial workplace and will not tolerate harassment of any kind. This includes sexual harassment, unwelcome conduct, threats or bullying, name-calling, negative stereotyping, unwelcome physical contact, offensive gestures, or damaging the personal property of others.
- ☐ **Workplace safety:** Under Armour is committed to preventing workplace violence and maintaining a safe work environment; there is zero tolerance for workplace violence.
- ☐ **Social relationships:** Under Armour wants to avoid misunderstandings, complaints, perceptions of favoritism, possible sexual harassment claims, adverse impact on morale, and disruption to the workplace that can result from relationships between a manager and a teammates he/she supervises. In the U.S. these relationships must be disclosed to human resources and the manager and teammate must abide by the Social and Romantic Relationships Policy in the teammate handbook.

☐ **Data Privacy**
- ☐ **Consumers:** Under Armour is committed to protecting the privacy of their customers everywhere and their privacy policies address the commitment to collecting, storing and using customer information. These are in accordance with all applicable laws. If there is a known or suspect data incident, the Privacy team can be contacted at dataissue@underarmour.com.
- ☐ **Teammates:** Under Armour collects and uses teammate's personal information as outlined in the Data Privacy Policy for Employees and Employee Candidates.

☐ **Protection of Under Armour Assets**
- ☐ **Confidential information and intellectual property:** It is important to maintain the confidentiality of Under Armour's non-public business and proprietary information. this includes any information produced while working for the company or information about products, marketing, customers, teammates vendors, contracts, businesses strategies, finances, manufacturing, designs, any unpublished data and reports, and intellectual property both during and after employment with the company. It is the responsibility of each teammate with access to confidential information to ensure it is only used for authorized purposes and protect it from theft, unauthorized disclosure and inappropriate use. Questions should be directed to the Legal team.
- ☐ **Computer and device use:** Teammates are responsible for appropriate use and protection of the Under Armour Network, company issued equipment, passwords, email and mobile devices, data, and company digital IP. The listed are meant to be used for legitimate business purposes only. Questions should be directed to the Acceptable Usage Policy.
- ☐ **Physical assets:** Teammates are responsible for protecting the company's physical assets. Any teammate who engages in theft, fraud or embezzlement will be subject to disciplinary action up to and including termination of employment and/or criminal prosecution. of Under Armour's non-public business and proprietary information; this includes information produced while working for Under Armour and information about products, marketing, customers, teammates (without consent), vendors, contracts, business strategies, finances, manufacturing, designs, any unpublished data and reports and Under Armour's intellectual property both during and after employment with the company. It is the responsibility of each teammate who has access to confidential

information to ensure that it is used only for authorized purposes like theft, unauthorized disclosure and inappropriate use. There may be cases when there is a legitimate business needed to disclose confidential Under Armour information or when a potential business contact needs to disclose their confidential information to Under Armour. In these cases, contact the Legal team prior to the disclosure of such information to obtain a Non-Disclosure Agreement. Please contact with Legal team with any questions.

- Computer and Device Use: Teammates are responsible for appropriate use and protection of the Under Armour network, company-issued computer equipment, passwords, email and mobile devices, Under Armour data and digital IP. These are intended to be used for legitimate business purposes only. If you have any questions, please read Under Amour's Acceptable Use Policy on Our House.
- Physical assets: Teammates are responsible for protecting physical assets, like stores and products. Any teammate that engages in theft, fraud or embezzlement with be subject to disciplinary action, up to and including termination of employment and/or criminal prosecution.

- **Media**
    - **Social media:** When online, please always remember the Social Media Policy on Our House. Do not speak on behalf of Under Armour on your personal media accounts and always keep in mind confidential company matters and the protection of others.
    - **Communications with the media**: Teammates should speak with their managers and the Brand's Global Communications team before responding to media inquiries or publicly publishing anything on behalf of the brand. Under Armour's goal is to put as much thought and effort into public communication as the company does in marketing campaigns. This allows the company to guard the strength of the brain by maintaining a consistent and accurate message across all communications. Unless authorized, teammates should not respond to any inquiries from analysts or investors--those should be referred to Investor Relations. This includes, but is not limited to, posting information on social media, message boards, chat rooms, blogs or other online media.

- **Gifts:** Relationships built with business partners are built on trust, value, quality and service. It is imperative to avoid even the appearance that any business decision is based on improper payments, favors, gifts or hospitality. Under Armour may give or accept gifts from business partners like products, services, travel and entertainment of model value (less than $200). Teammates may never solicit gift, gratuities, meals or entertainment. Any gift valued at over $200 requires guidance and approval from the leader of your business unit or Global Ethics & Compliance. Giving or receiving cash equivalents is not permitted.

- **Recordkeeping**
    - **Reimbursement of expenses:** All business expense transactions incurred by individual teammates for spends like transportation, hotel, meals and entertainment must be promptly documented, recorded accurately and be in compliance with our policies and procedures. False or inflated expenses will result in disciplinary action, up to and including termination of employment and potentially criminal prosecution, regardless of the date of discovery. Personal expenses and business expenses should always be separated. Always err on the side of being conservative. Contact your manager with questions, or reference the Travel and Entertainment Policy on Our House for more information. Be especially careful when dealing with government personnel (see our Anti-Corruption Compliance Policy) and student-athletes (contact the Legal Team).

- **Accurate reports and records**: We strive for fairness and accuracy in all our records and reports. Teammates may not make any false statements, misleading entries or material omissions in any of Under Armour's books, financial records, personnel records and systems or other documents or communications. Since Under Armour's shares are publicly traded, we're obligated to make full, fair, timely, compliant, accurate and understandable disclosures to the public. All teammates responsible for the preparation of our public disclosures, or who provide information as part of that process, have a responsibility to ensure that these disclosures and information are complete, accurate and in compliance with our disclosure controls and procedures.. If a supervisor asks you to record incomplete or inaccurate information into our books or records, you must report it to the highest level of management on your team, the Human Resources department, Global Ethics & Compliance or the hotline.

- **Honest and fair dealing:**
  - **General:** We must be fair and honest in our business dealings with everyone, including customers, suppliers, employees and competitors. We gain our competitive advantages because we Tell a Great Story, Make a Great Product, and Provide Great Service. As teammates, we must not win business through unethical practices, false advertising or by disparaging the competition. While fair dealing laws vary for each country, breaches may result in criminal prosecution or fines. It is important for each teammate to be aware of and adhere to the relevant laws, regulations and requirements.
  - **Antitrust:** We grow our business while taking care to comply with the antitrust and competition laws around the globe. Generally, these laws prohibit discussions, arrangements, understandings or agreements among competitors regarding price or restriction of market, and between UA and its retailers to maintain retail prices. Remove yourself from conversations on these topics and let your manager or the Legal Team know if you have any concerns. Penalties for violating these laws include severe fines for UA as well as potential criminal charges for any teammate involved. For additional questions regarding competition and antitrust issues, contact the Legal Team.
  - **Make the right call:** Don't discuss prices, agree to set prices or maintain retail price, share confidential information, or agree with our competitors to limit or restrict market share with.

- **Insider trading**: While at Under Armour, you may come to possess material information about Under Armour or other companies with which we do business that is not available to the public. including information that a reasonable investor would consider important in deciding whether to buy, sell, or hold the securities involved, or any information that would, if disclosed to the public, likely affect the market price of the securities. This can include both positive and negative information. Information is generally considered public if the information has been spread through a press release, SEC filing, or other wide public distribution. It is illegal for you to buy or sell stock or other securities of Under Armour or any company with which we do business while you are in possession of material nonpublic information. It is also illegal for you to disclose such information to anyone else, including members of your immediate family or household, who might buy or sell securities in response to such information, or to suggest to anyone else that they buy or sell securities of the relevant company. Any of the conduct discussed above can result in severe disciplinary action, up to and including termination of your employment, and subject both you and Under Armour to civil liability and criminal prosecution. Under Armour's Insider Trading Policy also prohibits you from effecting short sales of Under Armour securities and from purchasing or selling derivative securities, such as puts and calls, relating to Under Armour stock.

- ☐ **Trading blackout periods**: As described above, at no time may you buy or sell stock or other securities of Under Armour or any company with which we do business while you are in possession of material nonpublic information. In addition to this general prohibition, there are certain "Trading Blackout Periods" during which you are prohibited from buying or selling Under Armour securities even if you do not possess material nonpublic information. Refer to our Insider Trading Policy for more details regarding the above, including when the Trading

- ☐ **Anti-bribery and anti-corruption:** Under Armour is committed to conducting business free from corrupt practices. We must comply with all applicable anti-corruption laws and regulations. This includes the FCPA and UK Bribery Act; no Under Armour personnel may offer, pay, promise to pay, or authorize the payment of anything of value to a government official or commercial partner to sway that person to act in any way to help Under Armour gain or retain business. This includes excess gifts, travel, meals, entertainment or other hospitality expenses, contributions to a political party, campaign or campaign official, and charitable contributions or sponsorships. This also applies to Under Armour's subsidiaries, divisions, associates, and agents. Violations of this policy may have serious consequences for both Under Armour and the teammates involved, including significant fines or criminal charges. Please review the Global Anti-Corruption Compliance Policy or contact Global Ethics & Compliance with questions.

- ☐ **Conflicts of interest:** We expect teammates wo avoid any outside interest that might conflict with their judgment or loyalty to Under Armour. Teammates should avoid outside employment or business or financial interests in another company that interferes with their job performance or their ability to devote their best efforts to their job. Teammates must disclose all outside employment or business enterprises in which they are involved as well as any financial interests the teammate or a member of their family has in any company that competes with or does business with Under Armour in accordance with Under Armour's conflict of Interest Policy located in Our House. Generally Under Armour will not do business with an entity in which a teammate or member of their family has an economic interest in (including employment) unless it has been disclosed in advance and the business is conducted at an arm's length and is deemed to be in the best interest of Under Armour. If you have reason or know of an actual or potential conflict of interest that may exist with respect to your interests and that of the company, you're required to disclose that conflict, in writing, in accordance with Under Armour's Conflict of Interest Policy.

- ☐ **Political process (for U.S. Teammates):** Teammates are allowed to participate in the political process as private citizens. Under Armour will not reimburse teammates for money or personal time contributed to the political campaigns; additionally teammates may not participate on a candidate's campaign during working hours nor use Under Armour facilities, resources, of their position in the company to advance any personal political issues. Under Armour, as a company, is prohibited for making contributions to candidates, officeholders, and political parties at the U.S. Federal level and under certain state and local laws in the U.S. Please consult with the Legal team, Human Resources team or refer to the Political Contributions Policy (uabiz.com) if you have any questions regarding political activity.

- ☐ **Corporate opportunities:** Each teammate owes a duty to Under ARmour to advance the company's legitimate interest whenever the opportunity arises. You must not benefit personally from the opportunities discovered through the use of Under ARmour's property or information or your position with the company or compete with Under Armour in connection with such opportunities.

- ☐ **Selection and use of third parties:** Third parties (including agents, consultants, and vendors) are expected to uphold our ethical standards. Before engaging with a third party, you should fully investigate and complete due diligence on the proposed partner. They may also be subject to comply with the supplier Code of Conduct.

- **Resources for asking questions and reporting concerns:** If you are aware of any conduct that is inconsistent with the Code of law, you can report it to the highest level of management on your team, the Human Resources Business Partner for your area or any senior leader in the Human Resources organization, or anyone on the Global Ethics and Compliance team (globalcompliance@underarmour.com). You can also phone the 24/7 hotline (listed below) or log onto Convercent.com/report to report any concern and anonymously if you wish. Information provided through the hotline and Global Ethical and Compliance team is directed to the United States and reasonable effort is made to secure personal data collected to avoid unauthorized use or disclosure such.
- **Hotline numbers:**

UA HOTLINE NUMBERS*

IF YOU ARE IN:	DIAL:
Australia	1-800-751-528
Austria	0800-802337
Belgium	0800-793-50
Brazil	0-800-591-8053
Chile	56-448906606
China	800-720-1113
Denmark	8082-6015
France	0805-080036
Germany	0800-183-3177
Hong Kong	800-906-573
Indonesia	001-803-015-205-5589
Ireland	1-800-948-640
Mexico	01-800-681-9259
Netherlands	0-800-022-0464
Panama	507-8339551
UK	0-808-189-0035
US or Canada	1-800-609-2574
Vietnam	122-80-385 or 84-444581777

*Phone numbers may
periodically change.
Please refer to Our House

Suppliers

As stated by Under Armour (2016), the following policies exist regarding its suppliers:

- **Values:** Under Armour's founding core values (innovation, inspiration, reliability, and integrity) set the standard for suppliers they choose to do business with. The expectation is for the suppliers and subcontractors to be consistent with the values, and additionally comply with the code of conduct, that treats employees in a legal, ethical and equitable manner. Under Armour seeks to do business with those suppliers and subcontractors that comply with the laws of the United States, the countries in which Under Armour products are produced, distributed, bought and sold, and the Code. Any violation of these laws or the Code may be viewed as a breach of the Manufacturing Agreement and could lead to the termination of the business relationship between Under Armour and the supplier.

- **Forced Labor:** Under Armour will not purchase products or components from suppliers that use forced labor; this includes prison labor, indentured/bonded labor, or otherwise.

- **Child Labor:** Under Armour does not purchase products that are manufactured by persons younger than 15 years of age, or younger than the age of completing compulsory education in the country of manufacture where such age is higher than 15.

- **Harassment or Abuse:** Under Armour's suppliers and their subcontractors must treat their employees with respect and dignity. Physical, sexual, psychological or verbal harassment or abuse is unacceptable and not permitted.

- **Nondiscrimination:** Under Armour does not permit suppliers and subcontractors that subject any person to discrimination in employment. This includes hiring, salary, benefits, advancement, discipline, termination or retirement, on the basis of gender, race, religion, age, disability, sexual orientation, nationality, political opinion, or social or ethnic origin.

- **Health and Safety:** Under Armour suppliers and their subcontractors must provide their employees with a safe and healthy working environment to prevent accidents and injury to health arising out of, linked with, or occurring in the course of work or as a result of the operation of employer facilities. Employers must fully comply with all applicable workplace conditions, safety and environmental laws and regulations. Where residential housing is provided to their employees, suppliers and their subcontractors must ensure that such housing is safe and healthy.

- **Freedom of Association and Collective Bargaining:** Under Armour suppliers and their subcontractors must recognize and allow the right of employees to freedom of association and collective bargaining.

- **Wages and Benefits:** Under Armour's suppliers and subcontractors must pay employees least the minimum wage required by local law or the prevailing industry wage (whichever is higher). They also must provide legally mandated benefits.

- **Hours of Work:** Except in extraordinary business circumstances, Under Armour suppliers and their subcontractors (i) shall not require their employees to work more than the lesser or (a) 48 hours per week and 12 hours of overtime or (b) the limits on regular and overtime hours allowed by the law of the country of manufacture or, where the laws of such country do not limit the hours of work, the regular work week in such country plus 12 hours overtime and (ii) be entitled to one day off in every seven day period. Under Armour suppliers and subcontractors must inform their workers at the time of their hiring if mandatory overtime is a condition of their employment. Under Armour suppliers and subcontractors shall not compel their workers to work excessive overtime hours.

- **Overtime Compensation:** In addition to their compensation for regular hours of work, Under Armour suppliers' and their subcontractors' employees shall be compensated for overtime hours at such premium rate as is legally required in the country of manufacture, or in countries where such laws do not exist, at a rate at least equal to their regular hourly compensation rate.

- **Environment:** Under Armour suppliers and their subcontractors will comply with all environmental rules, regulations and standards applicable to their operations.
- **Legal and Ethical Business Practices:** Under Armour suppliers and their subcontractors must be ethical and in their practice and fully comply with all applicable local, state, federal, national and international, laws, rules and regulations covering topics such as child labor, wages, hours, labor, health and safety, and immigration. Any company that determines to adopt the Workplace Code of Conduct shall also comply with and support the Workplace Code of Conduct in accordance with the attached Principles of Monitoring. The company shall apply the higher standard in cases of differences or conflicts. Any company that determines to adopt the Workplace Code of Conduct also will require its licensees and contractors and, in the case of a retailer, its suppliers to comply by the same standards.

Human Resources

Under Armour does not have a Human Resources policy made publically available on its website.

E. Strategic Managers and Board

Sr. Level Executives & Key Employees Biographies

Kevin A. Plank
Board: Executive Board
Job Title: Chief Executive Officer and Chairman of the Board Since: 1996
Age: 42

Mr. Plank was the specials teams captain of the University of Maryland football team. Tired of repeatedly changing the cotton T-shirt under his jersey as it became wet and heavy during the course of a game, Mr. Plank set out to develop a next generation shirt that would remain drier and lighter. He created a new category of sporting apparel called performance apparel, and built our Company into a leading developer, marketer, and distributor of branded performance apparel, footwear and accessories. Mr. Plank has been the Chief Executive Officer and Chairman of the Board at Under Armour since 1996. He also serves as a Director at the National Football Foundation and College Hall of Fame, and is a member of the Board of Trustees of the University of Maryland College Park Foundation.

A.B. Krongard
Board: Non-Executive Board
Job Title: Lead Director Since: 2006
Age: 78

Mr. Krongard has been the Lead Director at Under Armour since 2006. He was appointed a Director at the company in 2005. Mr. Krongard served as the Executive Director at the Central Intelligence Agency from 2001 to 2004 and as Counselor to the Director from 2000 to 2001. He previously served in various capacities at Alex.Brown, including as Chief Executive Officer and Chairman of the Board. Mr. Krongard was also the Vice Chairman of the Board of Bankers Trust. He is also a Director at Iridium Communications and Apollo Global Management.

George W. Bodenheimer
Board: Non Executive Board
Job Title: Director
Since: 2014
Age: 57

Mr. Bodenheimer has been a Director at Under Armour since 2014. Previously, he served as the Executive Chairman at ESPN from 2012 to 2014. Mr. Bodenheimer was the Co-Chairman at Disney Media Networks from 2004 to 2012 and the President at ABC Sports from 2003 to 2012. He served as the President at ESPN from 1998 to 2012. Mr. Bodenheimer also serves as a Director at Sirius XM Holdings.

Byron K. Adams Jr.
Board: Non-Executive Board
Job Title: Director
Since: 2003
Age: 60

Mr. Adams has been a Director at Under Armour since 2003. He served as senior advisor to the Chairman from 2013 to 2014 and as Chief Performance Officer at Under Armour from 2011 to 2013. Prior to joining the company, Mr. Adams founded and was a Managing Director of Rosewood Capital, a private equity firm focused on consumer brands, from 1985 to 2011.

Douglas E. Coltharp
Board: Non-Executive Board
Job Title: Director
Since: 2004
Age: 53

Mr. Coltharp has been a Director at Under Armour since 2004. He has also been an Executive Vice President and the Chief Financial Officer at HealthSouth Corporation since 2010. Prior to that, Mr. Coltharp was a Partner at Arlington Capital Advisors and Arlington Investment Partners from 2007 to 2010 and an Executive Vice President and the Chief Financial Officer at Saks Incorporated and its predecessor organization from 1996 to 2007.

Anthony W. Deering
Board: Non-Executive Board
Job Title: Director
Since: 2008
Age: 70

Mr. Deering has been a Director at Under Armour since 2008. He currently serves as the Chairman at Exeter Capital. Prior to that, Mr. Deering served as the Chairman of the Board and Chief Executive Officer at The Rouse Company from 1997 to 2004. He joined The Rouse Company in 1972 and held a variety of positions, including Vice President and Treasurer, Senior Vice President and Chief Financial Officer, and President and Chief Operating Officer. Mr. Deering serves on the Board of Directors at Brixmor Property Group. He also serves as the Lead Independent Director on the Boards at the T. Rowe Price Mutual Funds and is a member of the Deutsche Bank Americas Regional Client Advisory Board.

William R. McDermott
Board: Non-Executive Board
Job Title: Director
Since: 2005
Age: 53

Mr. McDermott has been a Director at Under Armour since 2005. He has served as the Chief Executive Officer at SAP since 2014 and Executive Board member since 2010. Prior to that, Mr. McDermott served as Co-Chief Executive Officer from 2010 to 2014 and as President of Global Field Operations and Chief Executive Officer at SAP Americas & Asia Pacific Japan. Prior to that, he served as the Executive Vice President of Worldwide Sales Operations at Siebel Systems from 2001 to 2002 and as the President at Gartner from 2000 to 2001. Mr. McDermott also served at Xerox from 1983 to 2000. He currently serves on the Board of Directors at ANSYS.

Eric T. Olson
Board: Non-Executive Board
Job Title: Director
Since: 2012
Age: 63

Mr. Olson has been a Director at Under Armour since 2012. He has also been the President and Managing member at ETO Group since 2011. Currently, he is also a Director at Iridium Communications, and Special Operations Warrior Foundation.

Harvey L. Sanders
Board: Non-Executive Board
Job Title: Director
Since: 2004
Age: 65

Mr. Sanders has been a Director at Under Armour since 2004. He was the Chairman of the Board of Directors, Chief Executive Officer and President at Nautica Enterprises. Mr. Sanders served as the Chairman from 1993 to 2003 and as the Chief Executive Officer and President from 1977 to 2003, until V.F. Corporation acquired Nautica Enterprises in 2003. He currently serves as a member of the Board of Directors for the Boomer Esiason Foundation for Cystic Fibrosis and the Starlight Starbright Foundation and as a member of the Board of Trustees of the University of Maryland College Park Foundation.

Karen W. Katz
Board: Non-Executive Board
Job Title: Director
Since: 2014

Age: 58 Ms. Katz has been a Director at Under Armour since 2014. She has also been the President, Director and Chief Executive Officer at Neiman Marcus Group since 2010. Ms. Katz joined Neiman Marcus Group in 1985 and has served in various executive and leadership positions, including the Executive Vice President of Stores, a member of the Office of the Chairman of Neiman Marcus Group, President of Neiman Marcus Online, and the President and Chief Executive Officer of Neiman Marcus Stores.

Kerry D. Chandler
Board: Senior Management
Job Title: Chief Human Resources Officer
Since: 2015
Age: 50

Ms. Chandler has been Chief Human Resources Officer at Under Armour since January 2015. Prior to joining the company, she served as the Global Head of Human Resources at Christie's International in 2014. Ms. Chandler served as the Executive Vice President of Human Resources at National Basketball Association from 2011 to 2014 and Senior Vice President of Human Resources from 2007 to 2010. Ms. Chandler also held executive positions in human resources at Walt Disney Company, including Senior Vice President of Human Resources at ESPN. She also held various senior management positions in Human Resources at IBM and Motorola.

Brad Dickerson
Board: Senior Management
Job Title: Chief Operating Officer and Chief Financial Officer
Since: 2015
Age: 50

Mr. Dickerson has been the Chief Operating Officer at Under Armour since March 2015 and Chief Financial Officer since 2008. Prior to that, he served as the Vice President of Accounting and Finance from 2006 to 2008 and Corporate Controller from 2004 to 2006. Prior to joining the company, Mr. Dickerson served as the Chief Financial Officer at Macquarie Aviation North America from 2003 to 2004 and in various capacities for Network Building & Consulting from 1994 to 2003, including Chief Financial Officer from 1998 to 2003.

Henry B. Stafford
Board: Senior Management
Job Title: Chief Merchandising Officer
Since: 2014
Age: 40

Mr. Stafford has been the Chief Merchandising Officer at Under Armour since 2014. Prior to that, he served as President of North America from 2013 to 2014, Senior Vice President of Apparel, Outdoor and Accessories from 2011 to 2013 and as Senior Vice President of Apparel from 2010 to 2011. Prior to joining the company, he worked with American Eagle Outfitters as Senior Vice President and Chief Merchandising Officer at The AE Brand from 2007 to 2010, General Merchandise Manager and Senior Vice President of Men's and AE Canadian Division from 2005 to 2007 and General Merchandise Manager and Vice President of Men's from 2003 to 2005. Mr. Stafford served in a variety of capacities at Old Navy from 1998 to 2003, including Divisional Merchandising Manager for Men's Tops from 2001 to 2003, and served as a buyer for Abercrombie & Fitch from 1996 to 1998.

Robin Thurston
Board: Senior Management
Job Title: Chief Digital Officer
Since: 2014

Mr. Thurston has been the Chief Digital Officer at Under Armour since 2014. Prior to that, he served as the Senior Vice President of Digital from 2013 to 2014. Mr. Thurston joined the company in 2013.

Adam Peake
Board: Senior Management
Job Title: Executive Vice President, Global Marketing
Since: 2014
Age: 46

Mr. Peake has been the Executive Vice President of Global Marketing at Under Armour since 2014. Previously, he was the Senior Vice President of Sales, North America and was the principal executive in charge of North American Sales from 2010 to 2014. He also served as interim Vice President of Footwear in 2009 and held various senior management positions in sales from 2002 to 2009.

James H. Hardy, Jr.
Board: Senior Management
Job Title: Executive Vice President, Global Operations
Since: 2015
Age: 55

Mr. Hardy has been the Executive Vice President of Global Operations at Under Armour since March 2015. He served as the Chief Supply Chain Officer at the company from 2012 to February 2015. Prior to joining the company, he served as the Senior Vice President of Operations at Hospira from 2011 to 2012 and as the Corporate Vice President of Supply Chain from 2009 to 2010. Prior to that, Mr. Hardy served as the Senior Vice President of Supply Chain at Dial Corporation from 2007 to 2009 and as the Executive Vice President of Product Supply at ConAgra Foods from 2005 to 2007. He also held various supply chain management leadership positions at The Clorox Company and The Proctor & Gamble Company.

Kip J. Fulks
Board: Senior Management
Job Title: President, Footwear and Innovation
Since: 2015
Age: 42

Mr. Fulks has been the President of Footwear and Innovation at Under Armour since March 2015. He served as the Chief Operating Officer at the company from 2011 to February 2015. Prior to that, Mr. Fulks served as Executive Vice President of Product in 2011 and Senior Vice President of Outdoor and Innovation from 2008 to 2010. He also held various senior management positions in Outdoor, Sourcing, Quality Assurance and Product Development from 1997 to 2008.

Karl-Heinz Maurath
Board: Senior Management
Job Title: President, International
Since: 2012
Age: 53

Mr. Maurath has been the President of International at Under Armour since 2012. Prior to joining the company, he served for 22 years in various leadership positions at Adidas, including Senior Vice President of Adidas Group Latin America from 2003 to 2012 and Vice President of Adidas Nordic from 2000 to 2003. Prior to that, Mr. Maurath served in other management positions at Adidas, including Managing Director of its business in Sweden and Thailand and Area Manager of sales and marketing for its distributor and licensee businesses in Scandinavia and Latin America.

Matthew C. Mirchin
Board: Senior Management
Job Title: President of North America
Since: 2014
Age: 54

Mr. Mirchin has been the President of North America at Under Armour since 2014. Previously, he was the Executive Vice President of Global Marketing from 2013 to 2014 and Senior Vice President of Global Brand and Sports Marketing at Under Armour from 2012 to 2013. Prior to that, he served as the Senior Vice President of Sports Marketing from 2010 to 2012. Mr. Mirchin served as the President of Retail and Team Sports from 2002 to 2005 and as the President of Team Sports from 2001 to 2002 at Russell Athletic. Prior to joining Russell Athletic, he served in various capacities at the Champion Division of The Hillshire Brands Company (formerly known as Sara Lee Corporation) from 1994 to 2001 and started his career with the NBA.

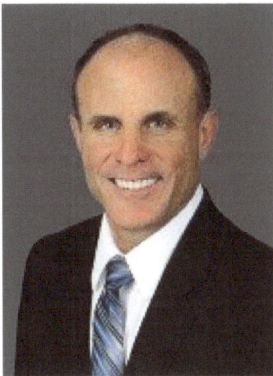

Lawrence (Chip) Molloy
Job Title: Chief Financial Officer
Since January 2016.

Prior to joining our Company, he served as Senior Advisor to Roark Capital Group, a private equity firm from October 2014 to December 2015. Prior thereto, Mr. Molloy served as Special Advisor to PetSmart, Inc. from June 2013 to April 2014, and had previously served as Chief Financial Officer of PetSmart from September 2007 to June 2013. Prior thereto, he worked with Circuit City Stores, Inc., and served as Chief Financial Officer of Retail from 2006 to 2007, Vice President of Financial Planning and Analysis from 2004 to 2006 and Director of Financial Planning and Analysis from 2003 to 2004. Prior to Circuit City, he served in various leadership, planning and strategy roles for Capital One Financial Corporation, AGL Capital Investments, LLC, Deloitte & Touche Consulting Group and the U.S. Navy. He served ten years in the Navy as a fighter pilot, later retiring from the Navy Reserve with a rank of Commander.

Corporate Governance

Responsibilities of the Board of Directors

The Board of Directors, which is elected by the shareholders, is the ultimate decision-making body of the Company, except with respect to matters reserved to the shareholders. The Board of Directors selects the Chief Executive Officer and certain other members of the executive management of the Company, who are charged with directing the Company's business. The primary function of the Board of Directors is therefore oversight - defining and enforcing standards of accountability that enable executive management to execute their responsibilities fully and in the interests of shareholders. Consistent with that function, the following are the primary responsibilities of the Board:

- Evaluating the performance of the Company and its executive management, which includes (i) overseeing the conduct of the Company's business to evaluate whether it is being effectively managed, including through regular meetings of the non-management Directors without the presence of management and (ii) selecting, regularly evaluating and planning for the succession of the Chief Executive Officer and such other members of executive management as the Board deems appropriate, including fixing the compensation of such individuals;
- Reviewing the Company's strategic plans and objectives, including the principal risk exposures of the Company;
- Providing advice and counsel to the Chief Executive Officer and other executive management of the Company;
- Assisting management in the oversight of compliance by the Company with applicable laws and regulations, including in connection with the public reporting obligations of the Company; Overseeing management with a goal of ensuring that the assets of the Company are safeguarded through the maintenance of appropriate accounting, financial and other controls;
- Appointing the members of and overseeing any required or appropriate Committees of the Board established for purposes of the execution of any delegated responsibilities of the Board of Directors; Establishing the form and amount of compensation for Directors, taking into account their responsibilities as such and as members of any Committee of the Board; and
- Evaluating the overall effectiveness of the Board of Directors, as well as selecting and recommending to shareholders for election an appropriate slate of candidates for the Board of Directors. In discharging their responsibilities, Directors must exercise their business judgment to act in a manner that they believe in good faith is in the best interests of the Company and its shareholders. Directors are expected to attend all or substantially all Board meetings and meetings of the Committees of the Board on which they serve. Directors are also expected to spend the necessary time to discharge their responsibilities appropriately and to ensure that other existing or future commitments do not materially interfere with their responsibilities as members of the Board. Directors shall be entitled to require that the Company purchase reasonable liability insurance on their behalf and to accord them the benefits of indemnification and exculpation to the fullest extent permitted by applicable law and the Company's charter and bylaws.

Structure and Operation of the Board of Directors

Size and Composition
The Company's charter provides that the number of directors of the Company shall be such as is from time to time fixed by, or in the manner provided in, the Company's bylaws. On an annual basis, the Corporate Governance Committee shall consider the size and composition of the Board and report to the full Board the results of its review and any recommendations for change.

There shall always be at least a majority of Directors that meet the independence requirements of applicable law, listing standards and, to the extent applicable, the Company's charter. A Director shall provide advance notice to the Chairman of the Board of his or her acceptance of an invitation to serve on the board of directors of any other public company. Directors who also serve as chief executive officers or in equivalent positions of the Company or other public companies should not serve on the board of directors of more than two other public companies, and other directors should not serve on the board of directors of more than three other public companies.

The Board of Directors is responsible for selecting candidates for Board membership and for extending invitations to join the Board of Directors through the Corporate Governance Committee. Candidates are selected for their strength of character, judgment, business experience and specific areas of expertise, factors relating to the composition of the Board of Directors (including its size and structure) and principles of diversity, including gender and ethnicity, among other relevant considerations, such as the requirements of applicable law and listing standards. The Board of Directors recognizes the importance of soliciting new candidates for membership on the Board of Directors and that the needs of the Board of Directors, in terms of the relative experience and other qualifications of candidates, may change over time. Any Director is free to recommend a candidate for nomination to the Board of Directors. Consistent with its charter, the Corporate Governance Committee is responsible for screening candidates (in consultation with the Chairman of the Board and the Chief Executive Officer), for establishing criteria for nominees and for recommending to the Board a slate of nominees for election to the Board of Directors at the Annual Meeting of Shareholders. Final approval of any candidate shall be determined by the full Board of Directors.

Each Director's continuation on the Board will be reviewed at the expiration of his or her term and before that Director is re-considered for election. In connection with its annual recommendation of a slate of nominees, the Corporate Governance Committee shall assess the contributions of those Directors selected for re-election. The Board of Directors does not believe that it is advisable to establish term limits for its Directors because they may deprive the Company and its shareholders of the contribution of Directors who have been able to develop valuable insights into the Company and its operations over time. A Director will, however, be expected not to stand for re-election after the age of 75. In addition, it is the sense of the Board of Directors that any Director whose principal occupation or business association has changed substantially from the time he or she was elected to the Board of Directors should volunteer to resign from the Board. While it is not the sense of the Board of Directors that such Director should in all cases resign, the Board believes that it would be desirable in such circumstances to consider, through the Corporate Governance Committee, the appropriateness of such Director's continued service. The Board further believes that Directors who are also employees of the Company should retire from the Board at the same time they relinquish their corporate officer title, unless the Board requests that such Director continue his or her service.

Consistent with its charter, the Corporate Governance Committee shall annually evaluate the performance of the Board of Directors as a whole. In developing its evaluation criteria, the Committee may choose to benchmark the practices of other boards of directors; circulate surveys, questionnaires and evaluation forms to Directors; and use such other methods as it may deem helpful and appropriate in order to assess the Board's effectiveness. At the conclusion of this process, the Chairman of the Committee shall report the Committee's conclusions to the Board of Directors and may make recommendations to the Chairman of the Board regarding changes that the Committee deems appropriate for consideration by the full Board of Directors.

Offices of Chairman of the Board and Chief Executive Officer
The offices of Chairman of the Board and Chief Executive Officer may be at times combined and at times separated. The Board has exercised discretion in combining or separating the positions as it has deemed appropriate in light of prevailing circumstances. The Board of Directors believes that the combination or separation of these offices should continue to be considered as part of the succession planning process. The Board further believes that it is in the best interests of the Company for the Board to make a determination as to the combination or separation of the offices of Chairman of the Board and Chief Executive Officer when it elects a new Chief Executive Officer.

The Corporate Governance Committee shall report periodically to the Board of Directors regarding succession planning with respect to the office of the Chief Executive Officer and other members of executive management as may be determined by the Board of Directors.

Lead Director
The intention of the Board is that one of the Company's independent Directors shall serve as the Lead Director. The Lead Director shall be elected by vote of the non-management Directors and shall be responsible for coordinating the activities of the other non-management Directors, including the establishment of the agenda for executive sessions of the non-management Directors, with or without the presence of management, as required by these Guidelines. The non management Director shall consider rotation of the Lead Director position from time to time. The name of the Lead Director or other means for persons to communicate directly with the non-management Directors shall be disclosed in the Company's annual proxy statement.

Board Meetings

Frequency and Conduct of Meetings
The Board of Directors shall meet at least 4 times a year, generally at 3 month intervals. Additional meetings may be scheduled as necessary or appropriate in light of circumstances. The Chairman of the Board shall, in consultation with the Chief Executive Officer (if these are separate individuals), the Corporate Secretary and the Lead Director, prepare an annual schedule of meetings for the Board of Directors and the standing Committees thereof. To the extent practicable, the schedule shall reflect agenda subjects that are generally of a recurring nature and are expected to be discussed during the year in question. Certain matters shall be addressed by the Board of Directors at least annually. These matters shall include a review of the Company's (i) strategic plan and the principal current and future risk exposures; (ii) strategic objectives; (iii) business and financial performance for the prior year, including a review of the achievement of strategic objectives; and (iv) compliance with applicable law and listing standards. The proposed annual schedule of meetings of the Board and its standing Committees shall be presented to the Board of Directors for approval.

The Chairman of the Board shall chair all meetings of the Board of Directors. The Chief Executive Officer (if a different individual than the Chairman of the Board), the Chief Financial Officer and Company counsel shall also attend all meetings of the Board, subject to the Board's discretion to excuse one or more of these officers from all or portions of any meeting.
Non-management Directors shall meet in executive session with the Chief Executive Officer at least once each year to discuss matters relating to management succession (including the Chief Executive Officer's recommendation as to a successor should he or she be unexpectedly disabled) and management development and to evaluate members of executive management. In addition, non-management Directors shall meet in executive session without management at each regularly scheduled Board meeting, and at least once each year only those non-management Directors who meet the independence requirements of applicable law and listing standards shall meet in executive session without management. Upon reasonable notice to the other non management Directors, any non-management Director may call for an executive session, with or without the presence of the Chairman, if the Chairman is also the Chief Executive Officer, or any member of executive management, if he or she deems it necessary or appropriate. In such circumstances, the non-management Director calling the executive session shall consult with the Lead Director as to the time, location and agenda for such

executive session. When meeting without the Chairman, any item proposed by any non-management Director may be included on the agenda upon reasonable prior notice to the Lead Director.

Agenda

The Chairman of the Board and the Chief Executive Officer (if not the same as the Chairman), or designee, shall establish an agenda for each meeting of the Board of Directors, which may include matters additional to those contemplated by the annual schedule of meetings of the Board of Directors. Directors may suggest the addition of any matter to a meeting agenda. Each Director may also raise at any meeting or executive session any subject that is not on the agenda for that meeting or executive session.

Information to be Distributed Prior to Meetings

Insofar as practicable, information to inform the Directors about the Company's business, performance and prospects and regarding recommendations for action by the Board shall be made available to the Board a reasonable period of time before meetings. Information should be relevant, concise and timely. Requests for action by the Board of Directors should include the recommendation of management and be accompanied by any historical or analytical data that may be necessary or useful to the Directors in making a determination as to the advisability of the matter.

Presentations

Materials regarding presentations on specific subjects shall generally be sent to the Board members in advance so that the Board's meeting time may be conserved and discussion time focused on questions that Directors may have. Where time or circumstances prohibit advance delivery of materials, the Chairman of the Board or his designee shall provide advance notice of the subject matter and the principal issues involved through an oral communication in advance of the meeting, followed by a complete presentation and discussion of the matter at the meeting.

Resolutions

The Board of Directors has adopted guidelines for the adoption of resolutions, which are included as Appendix I. Insofar as is practicable, the text of resolutions to be submitted to the Board of Directors for approval shall be distributed in advance of the meeting at which they will be considered

Minutes

The Secretary of the Company or his designee shall record minutes of all meetings of the Board of Directors and shareholders. In the absence or incapacity of the Secretary or his designee, the Chairman may designate an Acting Secretary, a Director or outside counsel for the Company to record the minutes of meetings of the Board of Directors or shareholders. With respect to any matter, a Director voting against a proposal may ask to have his or her dissent recorded in the minutes of the meeting, and the secretary for the meeting shall do so.

Access to Management, Management Information and Counsel

Directors shall have free access to management and management information. Management shall be responsive to requests for information from Board members. The Board encourages the Chairman of the Board to invite members of management to make presentations at Board meetings in order to provide particular insights into aspects of the Company's business or to provide individuals with exposure to the Board of Directors for purposes of management development. Directors may suggest possible guests to the Chairman. The Board of Directors, the Committees thereof and the Lead Director (on behalf of the non-management Directors as a group) shall be entitled, at the expense of the Company, to engage such independent legal, financial or other advisors as they deem appropriate, without consulting or obtaining the approval of any officer of the Company, with respect to any matters subject to their respective authority.

Board Interaction with Institutional Investors, the Press and other Constituencies
The Board believes that management generally speaks for the Company. Directors may, from time to time, be contacted by institutional investors, other shareholders, sellers of businesses or merger partners, governmental or community officials, analysts or the press to comment on or discuss the business of the Company. Directors are expected to refrain from communicating with any of the foregoing without prior consultation with the Chief Executive Officer or the Chief Financial Officer. Any proposed contact by a Director in response to any inquiry by any governmental official should also be notified in advance to Company counsel.

Directors may also, from time to time, discuss the Company's business with customers, suppliers and others. While Directors are free to engage in these discussions, they should advise appropriate members of executive management.

In no event shall any Director disclose any material non-public information concerning the Company. Among other considerations, such disclosures may violate applicable law. Questions about such information should be directed to the Company counsel. In the event that a Director inadvertently discloses information that may be material and non-public, he or she should immediately so advise the Company counsel.

Committees of the Board

Committee Structure
There are currently three standing Committees of the Board of Directors: Audit, Compensation and Corporate Governance. From time to time, the Board may designate ad hoc Committees in conformity with the Company's bylaws. Each standing Committee shall have the authority and responsibilities delineated in the Company's bylaws, the resolutions creating them and any applicable charter. The Board of Directors shall have the authority to disband any ad hoc or standing Committee when it deems it appropriate to do so, provided that the Company shall at all times have Audit, Compensation and Corporate Governance Committees and such other Committees as may be required by applicable law or listing standards.

Committees and their Chairpersons shall be appointed by the Board of Directors annually at the Annual Meeting of the Board of Directors, on recommendation of the Corporate Governance Committee in consultation with the Chairman of the Board. The members of the Audit, Compensation and Corporate Governance Committees shall at all times meet the independence and other requirements of applicable law and listing requirements. In appointing Committee members, the Board shall consider rotating membership from time to time in accordance with any policies established or recommended in that regard by the Corporate Governance Committee.

If any member of the Audit Committee simultaneously serves on the audit committees of more than three public companies, so long as the Company does not limit the number of other audit committees on which the Audit Committee's members may simultaneously serve, then, in each such case, the Board of Directors shall determine that such simultaneous service will not impair the ability of such member to effectively serve on the Audit Committee.

Each standing Committee shall have a written charter, which shall be approved by the full Board of Directors and state the purpose of such Committee. Committee charters shall be reviewed not less frequently than annually to reflect the activities of each of the respective Committees changes in applicable law or regulation and other relevant considerations, and proposed revisions to such charters shall be approved by the full Board of Directors.

Committee Meetings

The Chairpersons of the various Committees, in consultation with their Committee members, shall determine the frequency and length of Committee meetings. The Chairperson of each Committee, in consultation with appropriate Company officers, will establish the agenda for each Committee meeting. Committee members and other Directors may suggest the addition of any matter to the agenda for any Committee meeting upon reasonable notice to the Committee Chairperson.

To the extent practicable, information regarding matters to be considered at Committee meetings shall be distributed to Committee members a reasonable period of time before such meetings. Each Committee Chairperson shall designate an individual of his or her choice to act as Secretary at, and to record the minutes of, Committee meetings. The Chairperson of each Committee shall report on the activities of the Committee to the Board of Directors following Committee meetings, and minutes of Committee meetings shall be distributed to all Directors for their information.

Compensation of the Board of Directors

The Compensation Committee is charged with the responsibility of reviewing the compensation of the Board of Directors and recommending changes thereto to the full Board of Directors from time to time. In this regard, the Committee may request that management report to the Committee periodically on the status of the Board's compensation in relation to other similarly situated companies. Directors who are Company employees shall not be compensated for their services as Directors.

The form and amount of Director compensation and perquisites shall be determined by the Compensation Committee in accordance with the principles contained in its charter or any related policies, and such Committee shall review the form and amount of such compensation periodically as provided in its charter. The Board of Directors continues to believe that an alignment of Director interests with those of shareholders is important. The Compensation Committee shall be sensitive to questions of independence that may be raised where Directors' fees and perquisites exceed customary levels for companies of comparable scope and size.

Director Orientation and Education

New Directors shall participate in an orientation program, which shall generally be conducted within two months of the Annual Meeting at which new Directors are elected. The agenda for the orientation program shall be determined by the Chairman of the Board, in consultation with the Chief Executive Officer (if different from the Chairman of the Board), the Chief Financial Officer, the Corporate Secretary and the Lead Director, who may consult as appropriate with the Chairpersons of the standing Committees of the Board of Directors. The orientation program shall address the Company's strategic plans, significant risk exposures, compliance programs (including its Code of Ethics and Business Conduct) and may include presentations by the

Company's executive management, internal auditors and independent auditors, as well as one or more visits to the Company's headquarters or other operating sites or facilities. All other Directors shall also be invited to attend each orientation program.

The Board of Directors shall encourage Directors to participate in continuing education programs, and the Company shall pay the reasonable expenses of attendance by a Director at such programs.

Audit Committee Charter

The Audit Committee assists the Board of Directors in fulfilling its oversight responsibilities to the Company and its stockholders by overseeing (a) the quality and integrity of the Company's financial statements, the accounting and financial reporting process, and the Company's systems of internal accounting and financial controls, (b) those involved in the preparation and review of the financial statements, (c) the performance of the Company's internal audit function and the independent auditor and (d) the compliance by the Company with legal and regulatory requirements, including the Company's disclosure controls and procedures.

Compensation Committee Charter

The purpose of the Committee is to approve, implement, administer and evaluate the Company's compensation plans, policies and programs for the directors and the Chief Executive Officer and other executive officers of the Company.

Corporate Governance Committee Charter

The purpose of the Committee is (i) to identify individuals qualified to become members of the Board of Directors, (ii) to recommend Director nominees for each annual meeting of shareholders and nominees for election to fill any vacancies on the Board of Directors, (iii) to develop and recommend to the Board of Directors a set of corporate governance guidelines applicable to the Company, and (iv) to oversee the evaluation of the Board and management.

Board Committee Composition

Board Committee Composition	AUDIT	COMPENSATION	CORPORATE GOVERNANCE
Kevin A. Plank ★		Member	
George W. Bodenheimer [I]	Member		
Anthony W. Deering [I]	Member	Member	
Karen W. tz [I]			Member
A.B. Krongard [I]	Chair		
William R. McDermott [I]			Chair
Eric T. Olson [I]			Chair
Harvey L. Sanders [I]		Chair	

★ = Chair of the Board   = Chair   = Member   [I] = Independent Director

Key Employee Compensation

Name	Job Title	Board	Compensation
Kevin A. Plank	Chief Executive Officer and Chairman of the Board	Executive Board	3556190 USD
A.B. Krongard	Lead Director	Non Executive Board	177500 USD
George W. Bodenheimer	Director	Non Executive Board	83750 USD
Byron K. Adams Jr.	Director	Non Executive Board	
Douglas E. Coltharp	Director	Non Executive Board	137500 USD
Anthony W. Deering	Director	Non Executive Board	137500 USD
William R. McDermott	Director	Non Executive Board	140000 USD
Eric T. Olson	Director	Non Executive Board	130000 USD
Harvey L. Sanders	Director	Non Executive Board	142500 USD
Karen W. Katz	Director	Non Executive Board	57500 USD
Kerry D. Chandler	Chief Human Resources Officer	Senior Management	
Brad Dickerson	Chief Operating Officer and Chief Financial Officer	Senior Management	1514777 USD
Henry B. Stafford	Chief Merchandising Officer	Senior Management	1792108 USD
Robin Thurston	Chief Digital Officer	Senior Management	
Adam Peake	Executive Vice President, Global Marketing	Senior Management	
James H. Hardy, Jr.	Executive Vice President, Global Operations	Senior Management	
Kip J. Fulks	President, Footwear and Innovation	Senior Management	1830130 USD
Karl-Heinz Maurath	President, International	Senior Management	3514378 USD
Matthew C. Mirchin	President of North America	Senior Management	

F. Generic Industry Type

Industry Elaboration (Fragmentation, Maturation, Energy, Growth) & Economics

Industry Definition

Under Armour, Inc. is considered part of the "consumer goods" sector, and most successful in the in the textile - apparel clothing industry yielding approximately 74% of its total sales (Statista, 2016; Yahoo! Finance, 2016). This industry consists of companies engaged in the manufacturing of clothing, such as men, women and children's clothing, uniforms, jackets, hats, socks, gloves, robes, hosiery and swim suits (New York Times, 2016). The company is also part of the footwear and accessories segments yielding approximately 14 and 9 percent of sales respectively (Statista, 2016). In order to gain a better understanding of the company's competitors, however, this report will focus on the athletic and sporting good manufacturing industry in which its key competitors reside.

Market Size and Growth Rate

The athletic and sporting good manufacturing industry is comprised of approximately 1,052 businesses, with $9.1 billion in revenue and $398.2 million in profits. The market has experienced a slow growth rate in the past few years due to a slow growth in sports participation. However, due to a changing market of more health-conscious consumers, the industry is estimated to grow at an annualized rate of 0.6% to $9.3 billion by 2020 (IBISWorld, 2015).

Key Rivals and Market Share

Key rivals are Nike, Inc. (NKE) and Performance Sports Group, Ltd. (PSG) holding 8.2% and 5.3% of the market share respectively (IBISWorld, 2015).

Scope of Competitive Rivalry

Using the Five Forces Model of Competition, the scope of competitive rivalry can be analyzed into the following categories:

- Supplier bargaining power is low. The supplier base is diverse and, therefore no single supplier holds a significant bargaining power.
- Substitute products is low to medium as demand is expected to continue. However, the problem of counterfeit products is an area for concern as they have been improving over the years and can threaten key players.
- Potential for new entrants is medium and steady. Large capital costs are required for branding, advertising, and creating product demands.
- Buyer bargaining power is low to medium. Big wholesale customers could exert bargaining power as they account for over half of key rivals' total net revenue. Also, customers can easily change brands on the basis of price, advertising, product sponsorship, and styles.
- Rivalry among competing sellers is medium to high. Competitions between established and upcoming sellers is growing and Under Armour does not hold patent for its products.

(IBISWorld, 2015; Trefis, 2016)

Concentration vs. Fragmentation

The industry has a low concentration level and is highly fragmented (IBISWorld, 2015; Thompson, Peteraf, Gamble, & Strickland, 2016). The top four players in the industry comprise less than 20% of the total revenue in 2015, but are using their branding to help gain more of the market share. Vertical integration helps an industry dominate the industry, very few manufacturers utilize this (IBISWorld, 2015).

Number of Buyers

- Buyer power is high
    - Switching to substitutes are low
    - Buyer is well-educated regarding the seller's products, prices, and costs
    - Buyer is price sensitive
    - Industry goods are standardized and differentiation is weak
    - Buyers have discretion to delay their purchases or even not make a purchase at all

(Thompson, Peteraf, Gamble, & Strickland, 2016)

Demand Determinants

- Price of related goods - There are many substitutes and traditionally, UA, have had limited patent protection on much of the technology, materials and processes used in the manufacture of our products.
- Income - During a downturn in the economy, consumer purchases of discretionary items are affected
- Effect of Advertisement - Marketing costs are an important driver of Under Armour's growth. Marketing costs consist primarily of commercials, print ads, league, team, player and event sponsorships and depreciation expense specific to our in-store fixture program for our concept shops.
- Expectation of Customers - If operations continue to grow at a rapid pace, UA may experience difficulties in obtaining sufficient raw materials and manufacturing capacity to produce products, as well as delays in production and shipments, as products are subject to risks associated with overseas sourcing and manufacturing. Expansion can also put strain on all available resources
- Weather/Climate - Under Armour expect to continue to experience, seasonal and quarterly variations in our net revenues and income from operations. These variations are primarily related to increased sales volume of products during the fall selling season, including higher price cold weather products, along with a larger proportion of higher margin direct to consumer sales. The majority of net revenues were generated during the last two quarters in each of 2014, 2013 and 2012, respectively. (SEC, 2015)

Degree of Product Differentiation

- Gearline Merchandising - Products are merchandised as gearlines that clearly communicate the conditions or uses for which they were designed

    ⬚   Three gearlines are marketed to tell simple story about highly technical products and extend across the sporting goods, outdoor and active lifestyle markets. Consumers choose HEATGEAR ® when it is hot, COLDGEAR ® when it is cold and ALLSEASONGEAR ® between the extremes. Within each gearline our apparel comes in three primary fit types: compression (tight fit), fitted (athletic fit) and loose (relaxed).

(Investor Relations: Financials, 2016)

Product Innovation

Product innovation and supply chain costs increased $82.4 million to $291.6 million in 2014 from $209.2 million in 2013 primarily due to higher personnel costs to support our growth in net revenues, along with increased investment in our MapMyFitness business. As a percentage of net revenues, product innovation and supply chain costs increased to 9.4% in 2014 from 9.0% in 2013 primarily due to the items noted above (Edgar|Company Filings, 2015).

Key Success Factors

⬚   Brand Image (registered and common law trademarks are important to differentiation)

⬚   Favorable intellectual property rights claims

⬚   Manage the integration of acquired companies and employees successfully

⬚   Grow the number of users, maintain or increase user engagement or ultimately realize expected revenues from our Connected Fitness community

⬚   Identify and originate product trends as well as to anticipate and react to changing consumer demands in a timely manner

⬚   Operating in markets outside of North America

⬚   Continued service of our senior management and other key employees

⬚   Attract, retain and motivate highly talented management and other employees with a range of skills and experience.

(Edgar|Company Filings, 2015)

Supply & Demand Conditions

The demand for this industry has seen a peak over the years as the population develops a more health conscious attitude and lifestyle.

Analysis of Stage in Life Cycle

The Athletic and Sporting Goods Manufacturing Industry is in the decline phase of the life cycle. The industry is failing to add to the overall global economy. In fact, the industry is expected to decline at an annual 0.7% over the next four years. During the decline phase, industries are facing more international competition. The market is saturated and sales and profit levels are suffering.

Pace of Technological Change

Technological change is slow in the industry. This is a main contributing factor of the decline phase of the life cycle.

Vertical Integration

Although few sporting goods manufacturers have vertically integrated operations, which include the manufacturing, designing, marketing and retailing process in operations, vertically integrated operations allow operators to dominate the industry. For example, Nike can use its retail establishments to modify pricing and examine consumer trends to implement new technologies and invest in research and development; other control a large market share.

Economies of Scale

Large companies enjoy advantages in economies of scale and brand recognition, and often offer a wide range of products. Small companies can compete effectively by offering specialized or unique products that interest enthusiasts.

Learning Experience and Curve Effects

The industry has a steep learning curve this is due to all the competition in the industry. The company is learning how to compete with Nike and make better shoes.

Barriers to Entry checklist

Competition	High
Concentration	Low
Life Cycle Stage	Decline
Capital Intensity	Medium
Technology Change	Low
Regulation & Policy	Medium
Industry Assistance	Low

SOURCE: WWW.IBISWORLD.COM

Barriers to Entry

Barriers to entry are medium and steady. Potential industry entrants have undergone barriers to entry over the past five years. Companies who have wanted to enter the industry will not because of certain barriers the majority of them being capital. Companies do not have the capital to invest in manufacturing and facilities. Other companies will not enter because of patents and innovation. The key industry players have a constant supply of capital and can invest in research and development to make new products. Other companies will not enter the market because of high marketing costs. They need to make their brand known in order to make a profit. The key industry players who have been in the industry for a long time already have this market presence. It would be the job of the new market entrants to shift customers over to their brand (IBISWorld, 2016).

Regulation/Deregulation

The level of regulation is medium and the trend is steady. Companies are subject to federal, state and local environmental and health and safety laws and regulations that impose workplace standards and limitations on manufacturing emissions. Additional regulations establish standards for the handling, generation, emission, release, discharge, treatment, storage and disposal of certain materials, substances and wastes.

The Consumer Product Safety Commission has established bicycle helmet safety standards and these manufacturing standards are required by law throughout the US. Helmets are required to pass lab tests to verify the helmet's integrity following drops and collisions from certain heights and distances. Straps and buckles are tested for strength, and foam barriers must be sturdily attached to the interior of the helmet.

Other regulations in the industry are often self-imposed through the industry's variety of trade associations. New golf club and golf ball products generally seek to satisfy the standards established by the USGA and the Royal and Ancient Golf Club of St. Andrews because golfers within their respective jurisdictions generally follow these standards. The USGA rules are generally followed in the United States, Canada and Mexico, and the R&A rules are generally followed in most other countries throughout the world.

Facilities within this industry are subject to extensive environmental legislation and regulations affecting the discharge of waste. Companies within this industry group are required to comply with environmental laws and regulations such as the Clean Air Act. Companies are also subject to occupational health and safety, wage, overtime, and other employment laws. Also, the Consumer Product Safety Improvement Act (CPSIA) has established safety regulations for products that are used by consumers aged 12 or younger. Products require frequent testing and if a product implements new technologies, or changes to the design, manufacturing process, component part or supplier, then the product needs to be retested. For manufacturers that provide products to young consumers, the CPSIA puts limitations on lead content.

Globalization

International trade is a major determinant of an industry's level of globalization. Exports offer growth opportunities for firms. However there are legal, economic and political risks associated with dealing in foreign countries. Import competition can bring a greater risk for companies as foreign producers satisfy domestic demand that local firms would otherwise supply.

Trade Globalization — Athletic & Sporting Goods Manufacturing

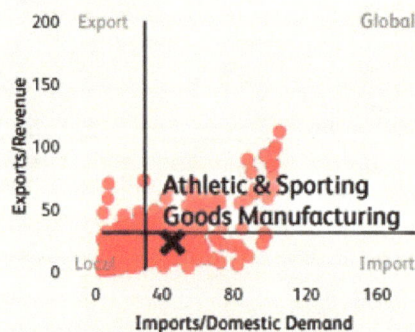

Going Global: Athletic & Sporting Goods Manufacturing 2003-2015

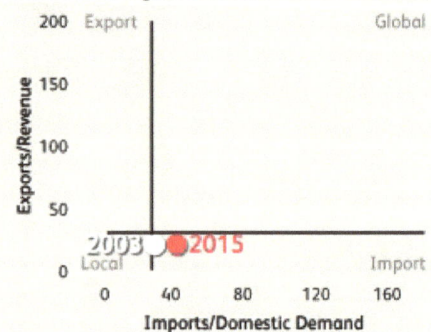

SOURCE: WWW.IBISWORLD.COM

Globalization in this industry is high and the trend is increasing. The Athletic and Sporting Goods Manufacturing industry is typified by a high level of globalization, with industry globalization expected to steadily increase over the five years to 2015. The rise has stemmed from growth in the number of companies that established subsidiaries in foreign countries. Many industry players rely on global manufacturers to provide input commodities for their manufacturing process.

Additionally, the industry has a significant number of firms that are globally based. The level of globalization will continue to increase in the industry due to global manufacturers' access to low-cost labor, particularly in emerging economies. Over the next five years, more manufacturing jobs will be moved to these countries, which can produce industry products less expensively.

Trends

Sporting and athletic goods at the manufacturing level is largely driven by trends at the retail level. Sports participation rates, which measure the percentage of individuals who participate in sports daily, provide operators with insight pertaining to consumer preferences within a community or state. As consumers allocate more of their leisure time toward sporting activities, demand for sporting equipment will rise.

Also, the growth and age structure of the population affects demand for sporting and athletic goods. The median age of the US population has remained fairly stagnant over the past five years. Trends for sporting goods is expected to decline over the coming decade, due to the aging of the population. While older individuals will adopt increasingly active lifestyles, this trend will be limited by more individuals having health conditions that may limit physical activity.

Sporting goods is also linked to seasonal trends, specifically weather conditions. The majority of sporting goods in this industry are for outdoor use. Weather conditions, such as longer summers, tend to encourage more outdoor activities, subsequently boosting demand for manufacturers. Seasonal changes create demand for different types of sport. Snow seasons create a strong demand for skiing equipment, while warm weather raises demand for golf equipment. To this end, the market for exercise equipment is highly seasonal, with peak periods occurring in spring and summer from late fall through February or the second to third quarter sales. As a result, the first and fourth quarters of every year are generally weak periods in terms of sales.

G. Organization Structure

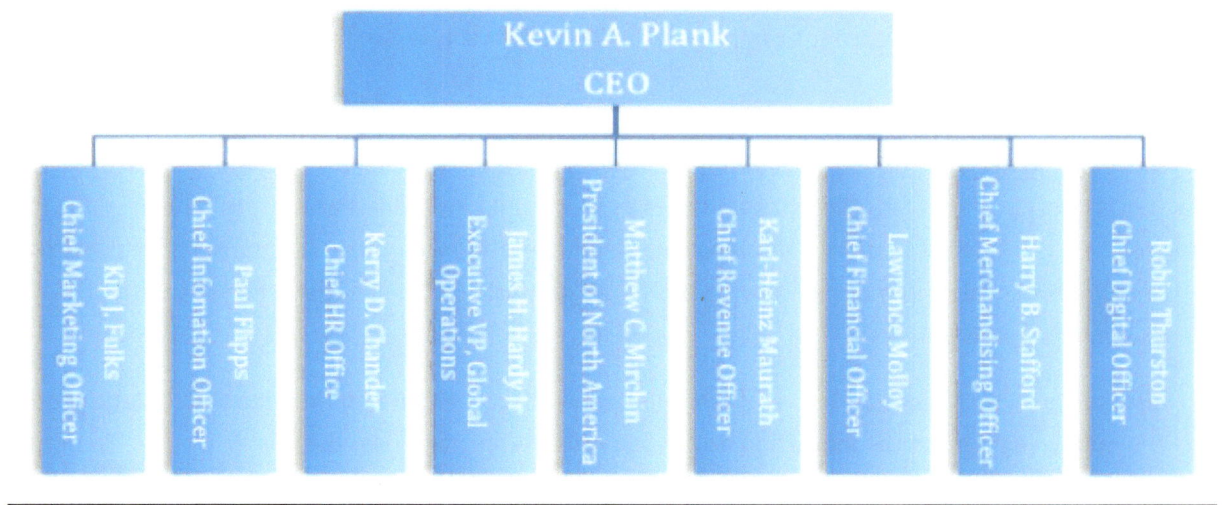

```
                          Kevin A. Plank
                              CEO
   ┌──────┬──────┬──────┬──────┼──────┬──────┬──────┬──────┬──────┐
Kip J.   Paul    Kerry D. James H. Matthew C. Karl-Heinz Lawrence Harry B.  Robin
Fulks    Phipps  Chander Hardy Jr  Mirchin   Maurath   Molloy   Stafford Thurston
Chief    Chief   Chief HR Executive President Chief     Chief    Chief    Chief
Marketing Information Office VP, Global of North Revenue  Financial Merchandising Digital
Officer  Officer         Operations America  Officer   Officer  Officer  Officer
```

Type
Under Armour operates under a functional organizational structure. In a functional structure, the organization is broken into functional departments, with departmental managers who report to the CEO and small corporate staff. Functional organizational structures are often referred to as departmental structures and unitary structures. The CEO and other chief officers are able to delegate their expectations and goals for departmental managers to deliver.

Advantages and Disadvantages
There are numerous advantages that are associated with functional organizational structures. One main advantage of operating under a functional organizational structure is that some of the pressure is taken off of top management. This helps enable more efficient use of managerial resources. Another advantage of the functional structure is greater task specialization. The promotes learning, enables the realization of scale of economies, and offers productivity advantages not otherwise available.

As with any business decision, there are disadvantages. The main disadvantage of the functional organizational structure is that departmental boundaries can often inhibit the flow of information and limit the opportunities for cross-functional cooperation and coordination.

Revenue by Business Segment

Under Armour operates under four main business segments: apparel, footwear, accessories, and licenses and other net revenues.

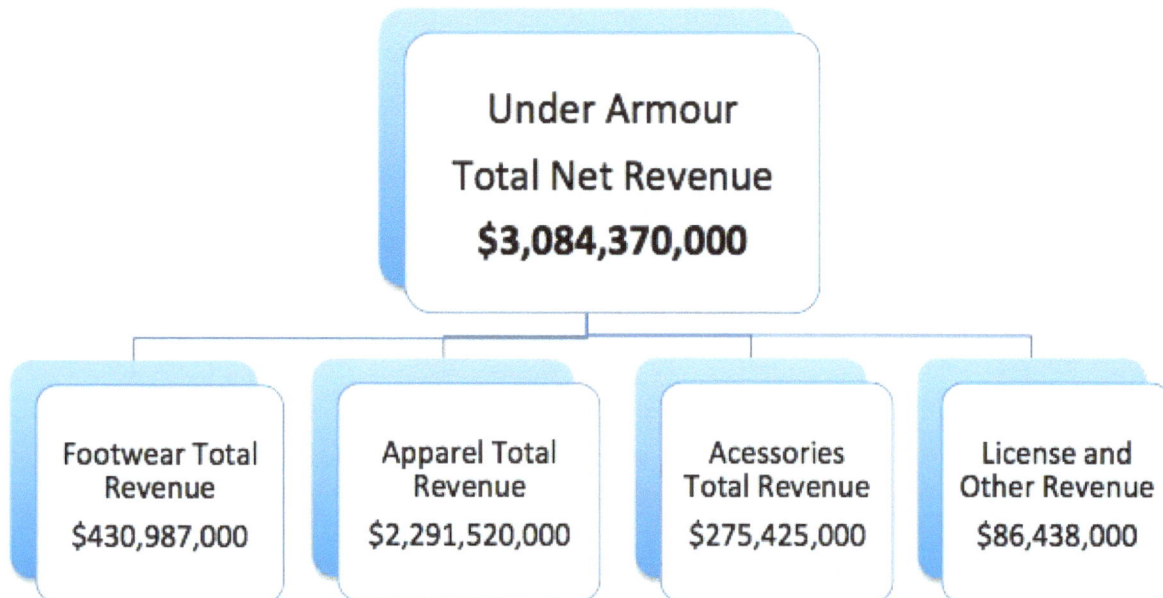

Under Armour
Total Net Revenue
$3,084,370,000

Footwear Total Revenue	Apparel Total Revenue	Acessories Total Revenue	License and Other Revenue
$430,987,000	$2,291,520,000	$275,425,000	$86,438,000

Source: Marketline Report

Revenue by Geography

Taking a look at Under Armour's revenue by geography, its FY 2013 sales totaled approximately $2.2 billion in North America (94.07 % of total revenue). Respectively, revenues for North America 2011, 2012, 2014 are approximately $1.3 billion, $1.8 billion, $2.8 billion (see below).Under Armour's other foreign countries business had revenues of 138 million (5.93 % of total revenue). Looking at its foreign countries revenues, Under Armour's 2015 10-K Annual Report states that its European headquarters are located in Amsterdam and the Netherlands and it maintains a Latin America headquarters in Panama.

UNDER ARMOUR, INC. SALES BY GEOGRAPHY

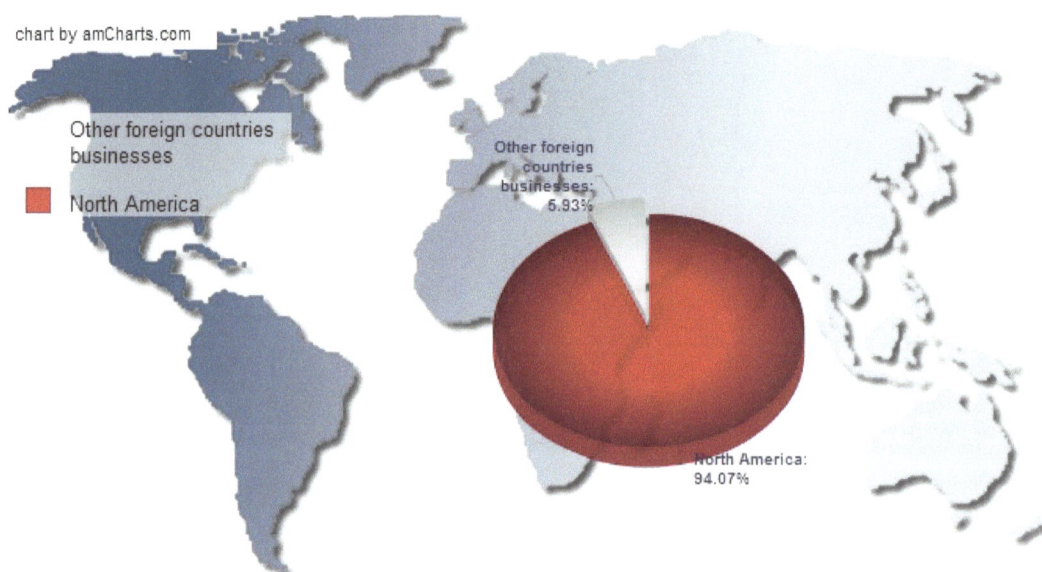

Geographic Inforamation		(Dec. 31, 2013) Revenues (in millions $)	(FY 2013) % (of total Revenues)	(Dec. 31, 2013) % Y/Y Revenue Change
North America	→	2,193.74	94.07 %	27.05 %
Other foreign countries businesses	→	138.31	5.93 %	27.84 %

Source: CSI Market

Under Armour, Inc., North America Division Sales

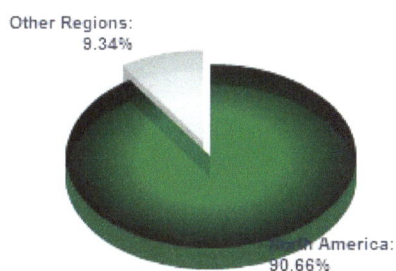

Revenue

Other Regions:
9.34%

$ 2,796.39

$ 2,193.74

$ 1,726.73

North America:
90.66%

$ 1,383.35

Percentige of Total Revenues

(FY 2011) (FY 2012) (FY 2013) (FY 2014)

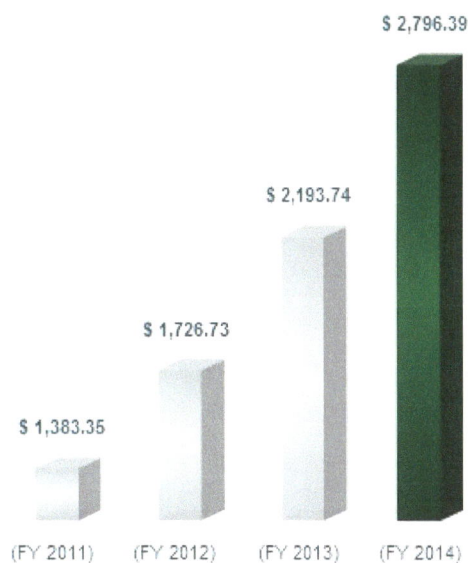

North America	(FY 2014) (Dec. 31, 2014)	(FY 2013) (Dec. 31, 2013)	(FY 2012) (Dec. 31, 2012)	(FY 2011) (Dec. 31, 2011)	(FY 2010) (Dec. 31, 2010)
Sales (In millions $)	2,796.39	2,193.74	1,726.73	1,383.35	0.00
% of total Revenue	90.66 %	94.07 %	94.1 %	93.93 %	–
Y / Y Revenue change	27.47 %	27.05 %	24.82 %	–	–

Source: CSI Market

H. Financial Analysis

Under Armour Key Ratios

KEY RATIOS	Unit/Currency	2014	2013	2012	2011	2010
Liquidity Ratios						
Current Ratio	Absolute	3.67	2.65	3.58	3.76	3.73
Quick Ratio	Absolute	2.4	1.55	2.32	1.99	2.28
Cash Ratio	Absolute	1.41	0.81	1.36	0.96	1.37
Leverage Ratios						
Debt to Equity Ratio	%	0.21	0.15	0.08	0.12	0.03
Net Debt to Equity	Absolute	-0.23	-0.18	-0.34	-0.15	-0.38
Debt to Capital Ratio	%	0.17	0.13	0.07	0.11	0.03
Efficiency Ratios						
Asset Turnover	Absolute	1.47	1.48	1.59	1.6	1.58
Fixed Asset Turnover	Absolute	10.09	10.41	10.15	9.25	13.98
Inventory Turnover	Absolute	2.93	2.55	2.99	2.34	2.48
Current Asset Turnover	Absolute	1.99	2.07	2.03	2.14	1.91
Capital Employed Turnover	Absolute	2.28	2.21	2.25	2.31	2.14
Working Capital Turnover	Absolute	2.73	3.32	2.82	2.91	2.62
Revenue per Employee	USD	717295.35				
Net Income per Employee	USD	48381.86				
Capex to Sales	%	4.56	3.77	2.76	3.82	2.84

Liquidity Ratios (Current Ratio, Working Capital)

Liquidity Ratios are a class of financial metrics used to determine a company's ability to pay off it short term debt obligations. Generally, the higher the value of the ratio, the larger the margin of safety the company possesses to cover short-term debt.

- **Current Ratio** - is calculated as current assets divided by current liabilities. An acceptable healthy current ratio, from industry to industry, is between 1 and 3. In particular, a current ratio of one (1), is not a good sign and indicates that company will be unable to pay off obligation if they came due at that point. The industry median is 1.97 for Global Apparel Manufacturing.

Current Ratio
Under Armour with Competitors

	Under Armour	Nike	Performance Sports Group
2011	3.76	2.85	1.98
2012	3.58	3.05	3.18
2013	2.65	3.47	3.81

■ 2011 ■ 2012 ■ 2013

Under Armour Current Ratio (10 Y)

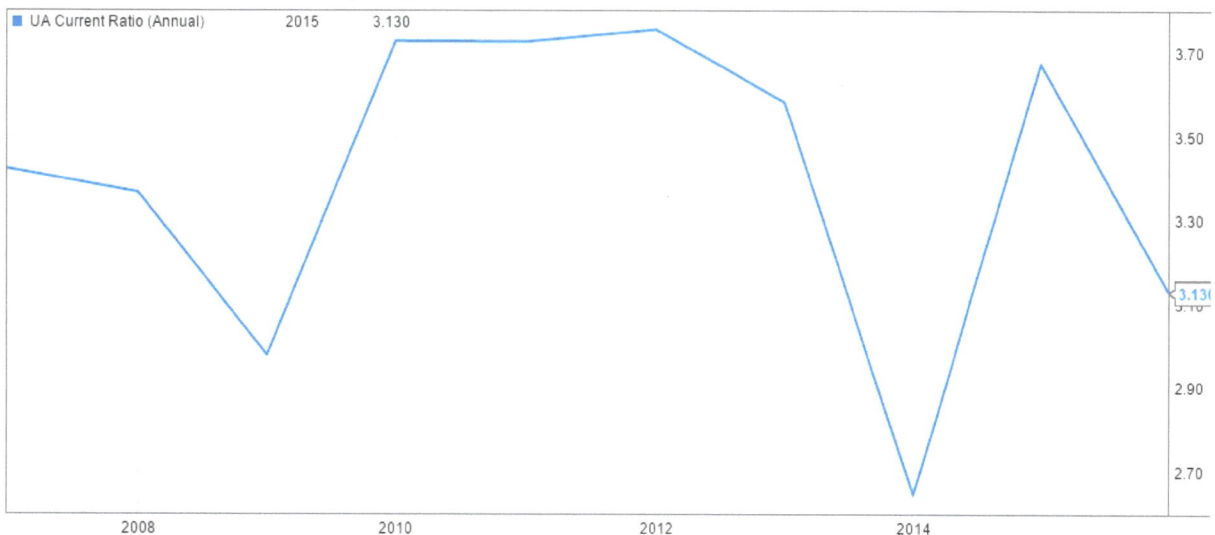

Source: https://ycharts.com/

As seen above, Under Armour's current ratio (10 Y) is currently above the industry median of 1.97. More, a current ratio above 3 does not necessarily mean that the company is in a state of financial well-being. This could mean that the company is not be efficiently using its current assets or its short-term financing facilities. This could also indicates problems in working capital management.

☐ **Working Capital** is calculated as the current assets minus current liabilities. It answers whether a company has enough short term assets to cover short term debt. The working capital ratio is calculated as the current assets divided by current liabilities. For the period of 2011-2013, Under Armour's working capital is $506.05 million, $651.37 million, and $701.48 million respectively.

Working Capital

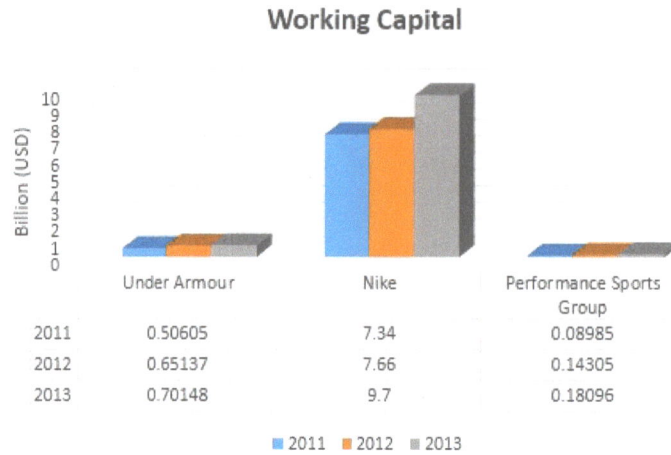

	Under Armour	Nike	Performance Sports Group
2011	0.50605	7.34	0.08985
2012	0.65137	7.66	0.14305
2013	0.70148	9.7	0.18096

■ 2011 ■ 2012 ■ 2013

Under Armour's Working Capital (10 Y)

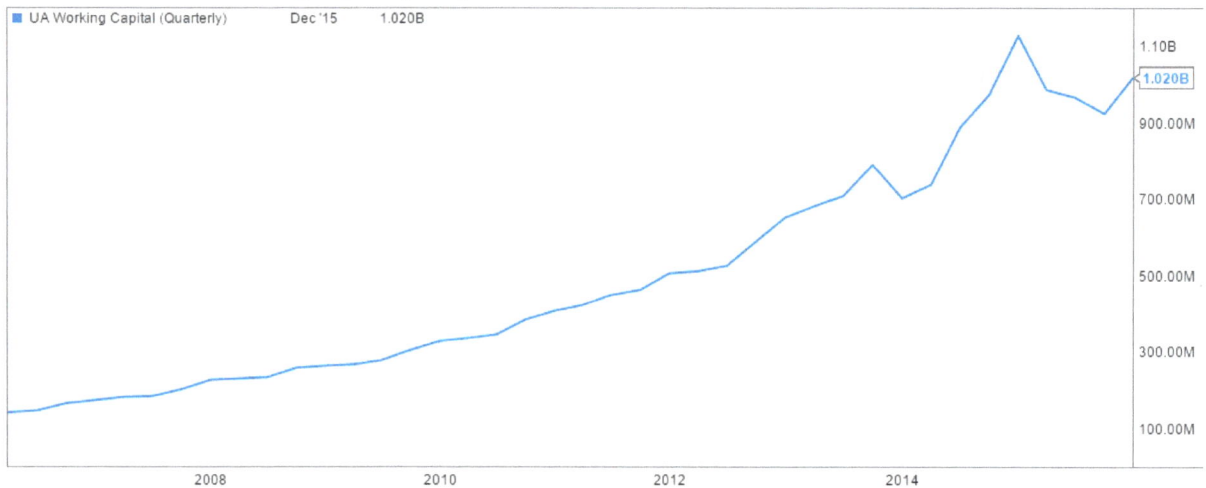

Source: https://ycharts.com/

VFC	NYQ	VF Corporation	2.15 B	
UA	NYQ	Under Armour Inc	924.51 M	
HBI	NYQ	Hanesbrands Inc	1.41 B	
MANDHANA	NSE	Mandhana Industries Limited	0	
RL	NYQ	Ralph Lauren Corporation	2.24 B	
LULU	NMS	Lululemon Athletica Inc	737.2 M	
PVH	NYQ	PVH Corp	1.49 B	
GIL	NYQ	Gildan Activewear Inc	872.73 M	
CRI	NYQ	Carters Inc	839.71 M	
COLM	NMS	Columbia Sportswear Company	962.84 M	

Data shows UA working capital is trending upward and is on par when compared with close industry rivals for FY15. They are just as likely to experience growth and improvement through the use of current available resources.

Source: https://www.macroaxis.com/invest/ratio/UA--Working-Capital

42

Activity Ratios/Efficiency Ratios (Days of Inventory, Inventory Turnover, Average Collection Period)

Activity ratios are accounting ratios that measure a firm's ability to convert different accounts within its balance sheets into cash or sales.

- **Days of Inventory [on hand]** - Measures inventory management efficiency. This is the average amount of time a company will hold inventory before the inventory is sold. Fewer days of inventory are usually better.

Days of Inventory

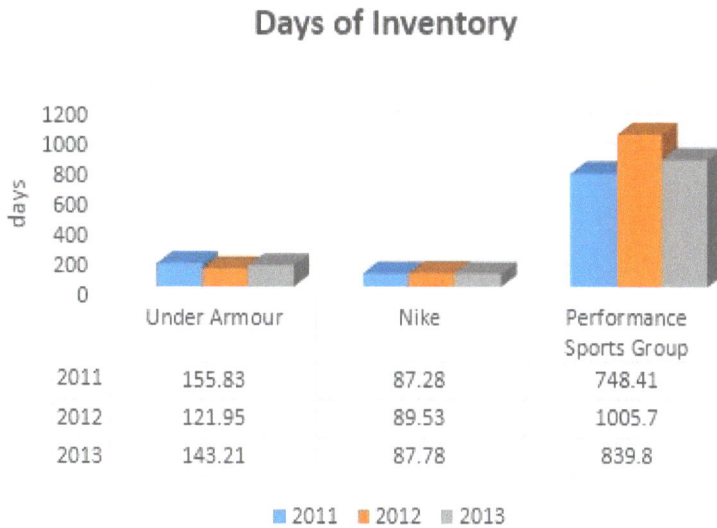

	Under Armour	Nike	Performance Sports Group
2011	155.83	87.28	748.41
2012	121.95	89.53	1005.7
2013	143.21	87.78	839.8

■ 2011　■ 2012　■ 2013

UA days inventory on hand is steady. Comparing year over year with Nike, UA should evaluate its lean practices.

- **Inventory Turnover** - Measures the number of inventory turns per year. Higher is better. The higher the inventory turnover, the less money the company spends on storage, write downs, and obsolete inventory.

Inventory Turnover

	Under Armour	Nike	Performance Sports Group
2011	2.34	4.02	2.6
2012	2.99	4.09	2.65
2013	2.55	4.16	2.6

■ 2011　■ 2012　■ 2013

UA Inventory items are moving slower than Nike. But, UA inventory turnover has been consistently above the industry average of 2.03

○ **Average Collection Period** - Indicates the average length of time the firm must wait after making a sale to receive cash payment. In other words, the average number of days between the date the credit sale is made and the date that money is received from the customer. A shorter collection time is better because it put cash in the company's hand to pay it bills.

UA is turning its receivables into cash quicker than Nike and Performance Sports Group. Is this good? UA must also compare this average against the credit terms they offer clients.

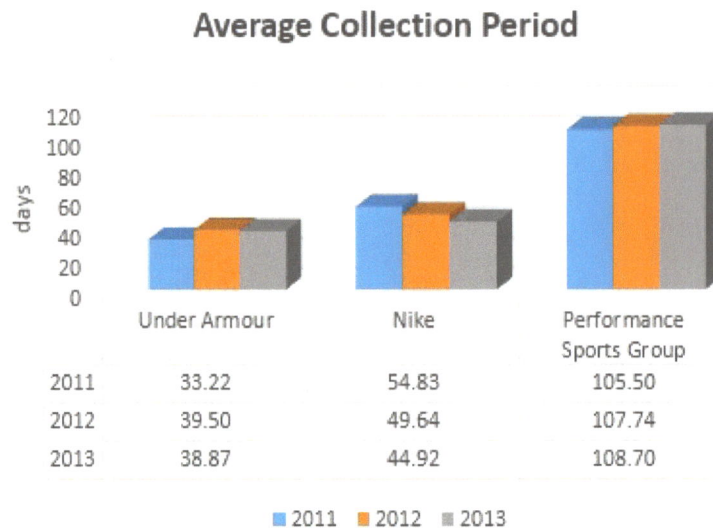

Average Collection Period

	Under Armour	Nike	Performance Sports Group
2011	33.22	54.83	105.50
2012	39.50	49.64	107.74
2013	38.87	44.92	108.70

■ 2011   ■ 2012   ■ 2013

Profitability & Growth Ratios

Profitability & growth ratios demonstrate a business's ability to generate earnings as compared to its expenses. Growth ratios detects consistency or positive/negative trends in a company's earnings.

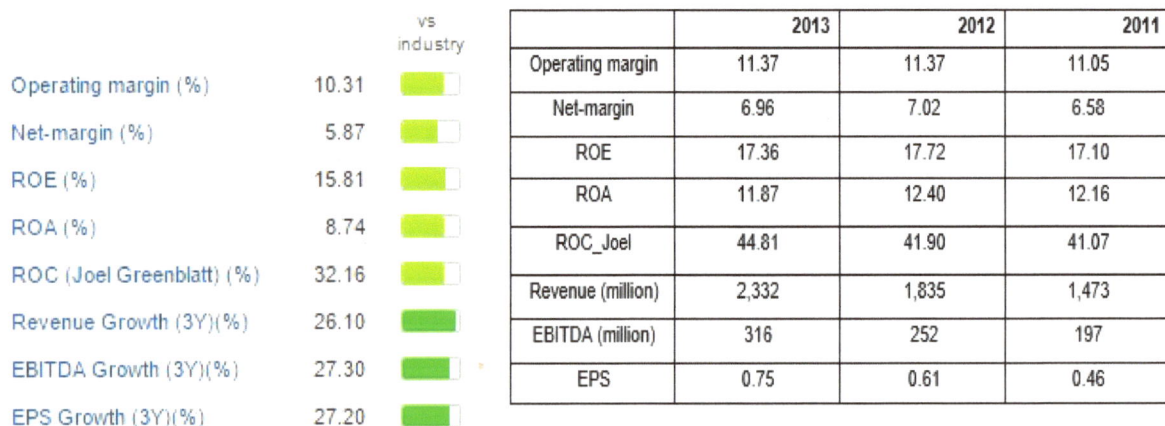

		vs industry
Operating margin (%)	10.31	
Net-margin (%)	5.87	
ROE (%)	15.81	
ROA (%)	8.74	
ROC (Joel Greenblatt) (%)	32.16	
Revenue Growth (3Y)(%)	26.10	
EBITDA Growth (3Y)(%)	27.30	
EPS Growth (3Y)(%)	27.20	

	2013	2012	2011
Operating margin	11.37	11.37	11.05
Net-margin	6.96	7.02	6.58
ROE	17.36	17.72	17.10
ROA	11.87	12.40	12.16
ROC_Joel	44.81	41.90	41.07
Revenue (million)	2,332	1,835	1,473
EBITDA (million)	316	252	197
EPS	0.75	0.61	0.46

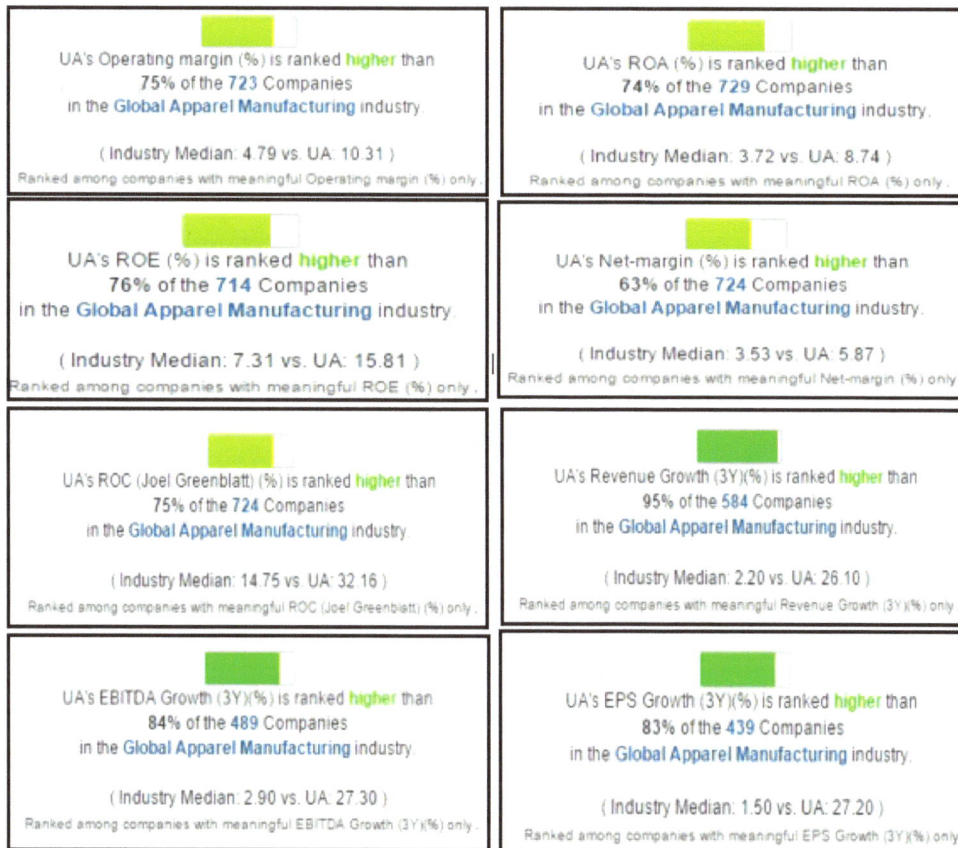

Source: (Gurufocus, 2016)

Summary of Profitability Ratios (refer to data above)

* **Operating margin** is steady. This should be watched closely as it will decline well before revenue or profits.

** The long term trend of the **Net-margin** is good indicator of competitiveness and health. How well are UA's revenues being converted into profits? Its net-margin is currently higher than 63% of 724 companies in the Global Apparel Manufacturing industry

*** **ROE** - How well is UA generating profit from every unit of its shareholders; equity? Desirables rates are between 15% and 20%. UA's ROE was above 17% for 2011, 2012, and 2013. It is currently at 15.18%. (See DuPont)

******ROA** - How well is UA generating profit from shareholder's equity plus its liabilities? UA current ROA is 8.74%. The industry median is 3.72% compared to UA (8.74%).

***** **ROC** - How efficiently does UA generate returns on the capital actually invested in the business? The industry median is 14.75% and UA median is 32.16%.

****** **Revenue Growth(3Y)** - UA's revenue growth is above 20% (3Y) classifying it as fast grower on Peter Lynch categorization of slower growers and stalwarts.

******* **EBITDA** - A measure of cash generation. UA's EBITDA '11-'13 was $197, $252, and $316 million.

******** **EPS Growth -** Earnings per outstandings share of company stock- $0.46, $0.61, $0.75 (yrs 2011-13)

Altman Z Score

The Altman Z- Score is the output of a credit-strength test that gauges a publicly traded company's likelihood of bankruptcy. Under Armour, as of February 22, 2016 is 9.42, indicating that is is in the Safe Zone. As seen below, when a Z- Score is less than 1.81, a company is in distress zone. And a Z-Score between 1.81 and 2.99 is the Grey Zone. The Safe Zone is above 2.99.

Source: (Gurufocus, 2016)

During the past 13 years, Under Armour's highest Altman Z-Score was 27.09. The lowest 4.54 and the median was 11.99. A competitive comparison (shown below) shows Under Armour's Z-Score when compared to Ralph Lauren, Columbia Sportswear Co., Hanesbrand Inc. and others.

Competitive Comparisons (Altman Z-Score)

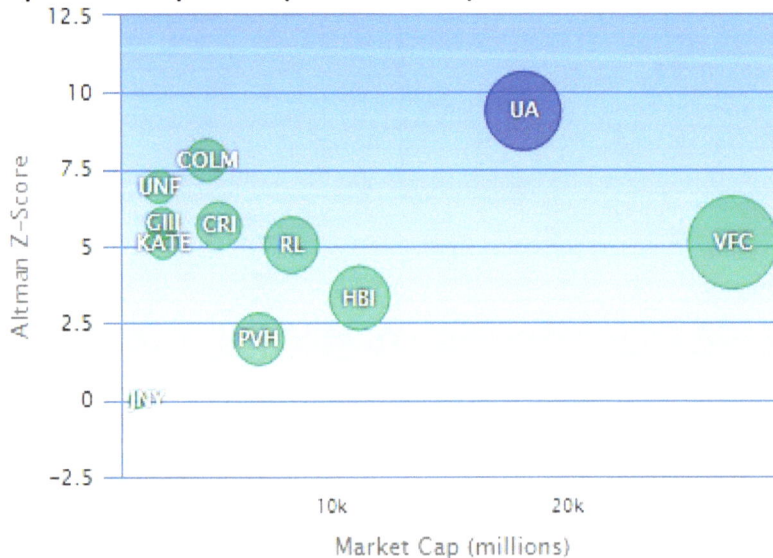

Source: (Gurufocus, 2016)

46

Tobin's Q

The Q Ratio is a popular method of estimating the fair value of the stock market developed by Nobel Laureate James Tobin. The Q ratio is calculated as the market value of a company divided by the replacement value of the firm's assets. As calculated, a low Q (between 0 and 1) means that the cost to replace a firm's assets is greater than the value of its stock. This implies that the stock is undervalued. Conversely, a high Q (greater than 1) implies that a firm's stock is more expensive than the replacement cost of its assets, which implies that the stock is overvalued. Overvalued is when a stock has a current price that is not justified by its earnings outlook or price/earnings (P/E) ratio and, therefore, is expected to drop in price.

Under Armour's Tobin's Q (10 Y)

Source: (YCharts, 2016)

Shown directly above, as of December 31, 2015, Under Armour's Tobin Q was 5.935. Previous Tobin Q values for the years 2011, 2012, 2013, and 2014 were: **2.909** (Dec. 31, 2011), **3.430** (Dec. 31, 2012), **4.887** (Dec. 31, 2013), **6.516** (Dec. 31, 2014).

DuPont Analysis

The DuPont Analysis analysis enables the analyst to understand the source of superior (or inferior) return by comparison with companies in similar industries (or between industries).

DuPont analysis tells us that ROE is affected by three things:

1.) Operating efficiency, which is measured by profit margin
2.) Asset use efficiency, which is measured by total asset turnover
3.) Financial leverage, which is measured by the equity multiplier.

Investors use return on equity (ROE) to measure the earnings a company generates from its assets. With it, one can determine whether a firm is a profit-creator or a profit-burner and management's profit-generating efficiency. A rising return on equity can signal that a company is able to grow profits without adding new equity into the business, which dilutes the ownership share of existing shareholders. As seen below, Under Armour's ROE has was steady over the years 2011, 2012, and 2013.

Under Armour's Historical ROE:

Historical Data

* All numbers are in millions except for per share data and ratio. All numbers are in their own currency.

Under Armour Inc Annual Data

	Dec06	Dec07	Dec08	Dec09	Dec10	Dec11	Dec12	Dec13	Dec14	Dec15
ROE	21.35	21.24	12.50	12.80	15.27	17.10	17.72	17.36	17.31	15.41

Under Armour Inc Quarterly Data

	Sep13	Dec13	Mar14	Jun14	Sep14	Dec14	Mar15	Jun15	Sep15	Dec15
ROE	31.59	25.41	5.01	6.29	29.76	26.94	3.43	4.22	27.24	26.37

Source: (Gurufocus, 2016)

**Under Armour 2013 - DuPont Model
($millions)**

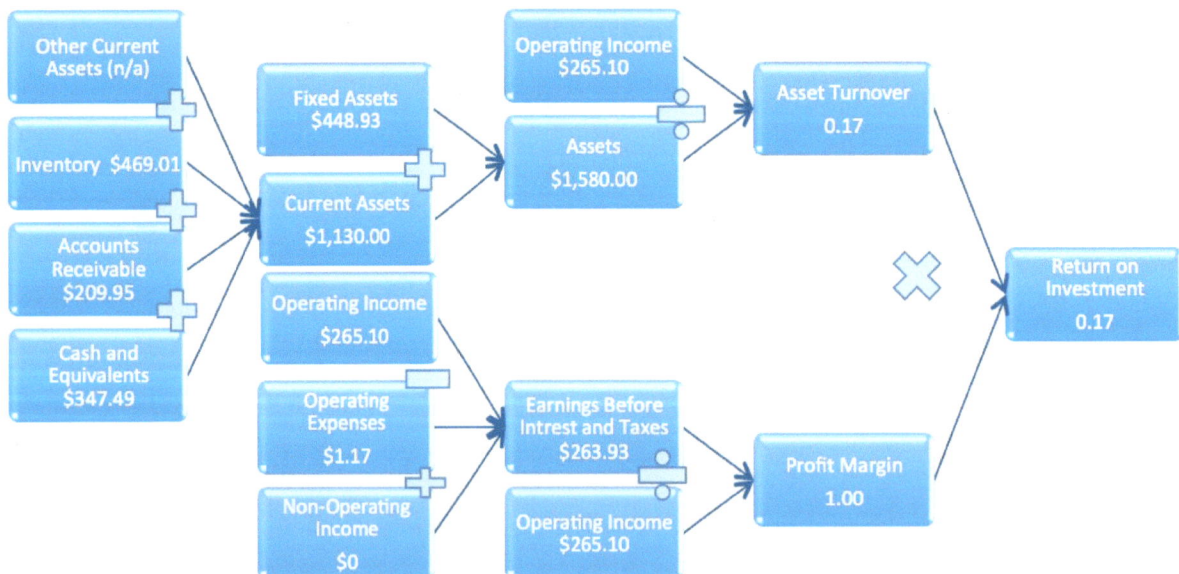

ROE Calculation (DuPont) - FY2013

		Return on Equity (ROE)		
Net Income	/	**Average Shareholder Equity**		
162,000,000		934,000,000		
(Net Income/Revenue)	*	**Revenue/Average Total Assets**	*	**(Average Total Assets/Average Equity)**
162,170,000/2,330,000,000		2,330,000,000/1,578,000,000		1,578,000,000/1,000,000,000
0.069600858		1.4765526		1.689507495
Net Profit Margin	*	**Asset Turnover**	*	**Leverage Ratio**
6.96%		1.4765526		1.689507495
Return on Assets		**Leverage Ratio**		
10.28%	*	1.689507495		
17.36%				

Under Armour's return on equity (ROE) has remained fairly steady with a slight decline between FY2012 and FY2013. This was due to the use of a slight increase in net profit margin and asset turnover and a slight decline in the leverage ratio. Respectively for FY2012 the net profit margin was 7.03%, asset turnover was 1.586 and the leverage ratio was 1.590. Despite the slight decline, it is ideal to see profit margin increase and leverage decrease.

Stock Analysis

3 Year Look (Source: Yahoo Finance)

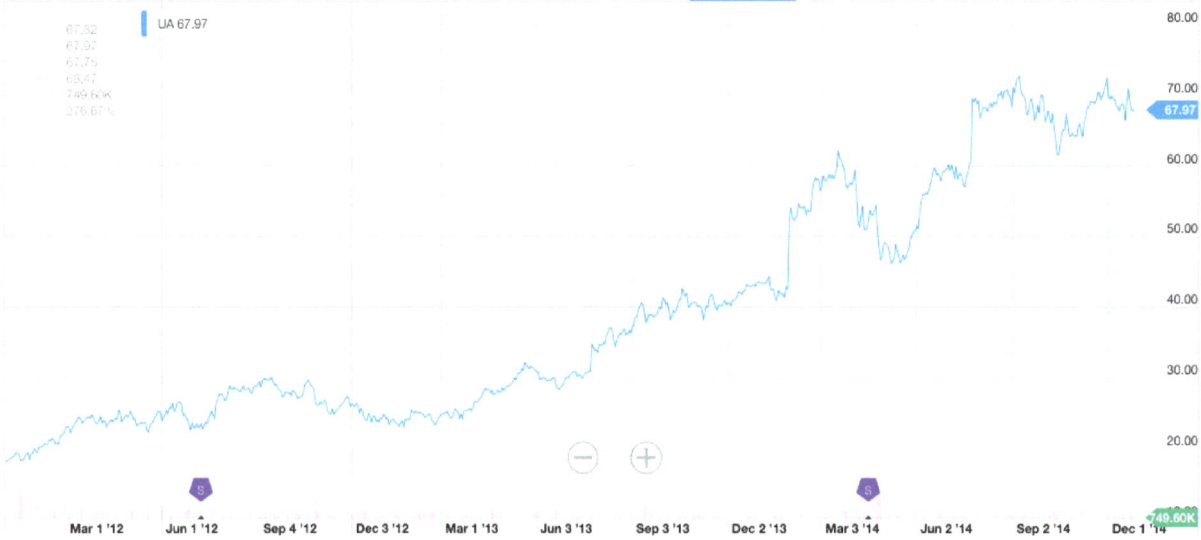

Under Armour trades on the NYSE under UA. In this stock analysis for 2012-2014, there is a marked increase in the stock price. This can be attributed to their growing market share of the company's three main business segments (apparel, footwear, and accessories).

I. SWOT Analysis

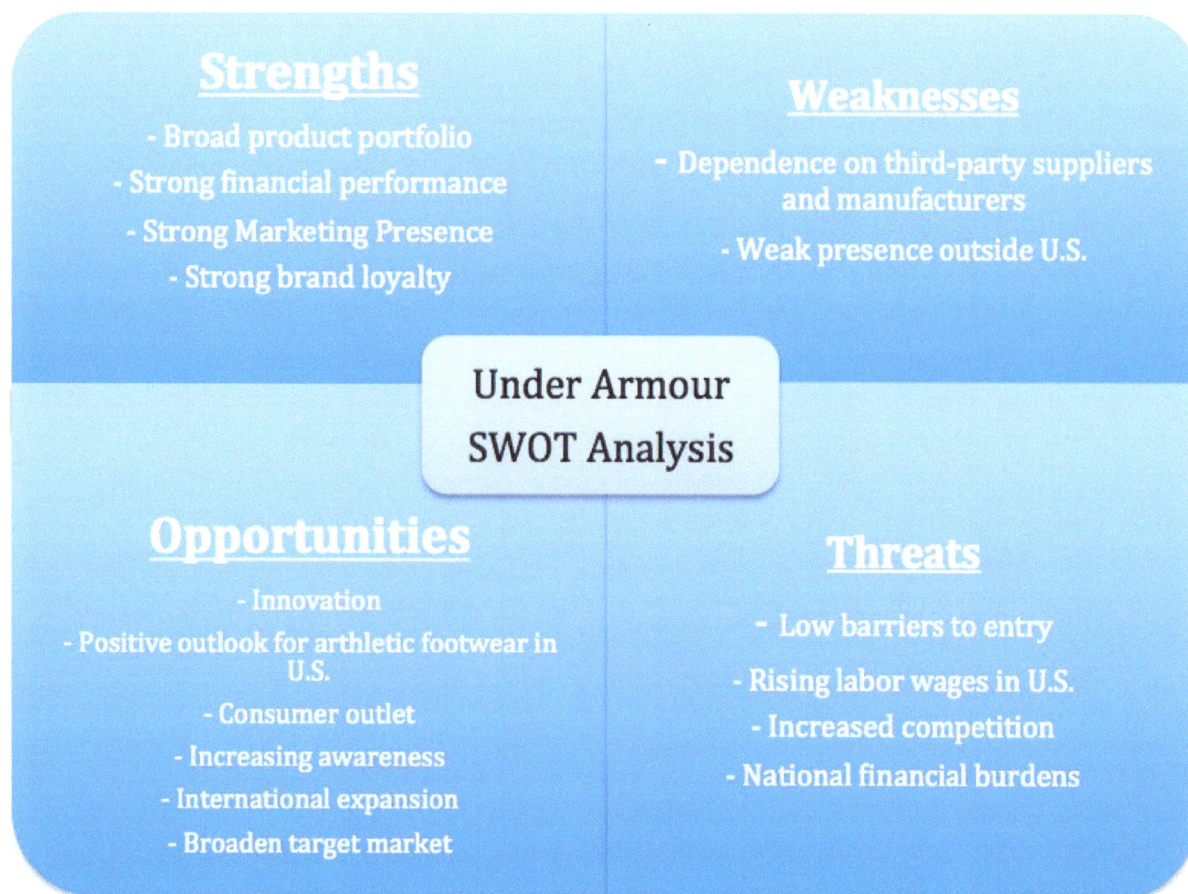

Under Armour SWOT Analysis

Strengths
- Broad product portfolio
- Strong financial performance
- Strong Marketing Presence
- Strong brand loyalty

Weaknesses
- Dependence on third-party suppliers and manufacturers
- Weak presence outside U.S.

Opportunities
- Innovation
- Positive outlook for arthletic footwear in U.S.
- Consumer outlet
- Increasing awareness
- International expansion
- Broaden target market

Threats
- Low barriers to entry
- Rising labor wages in U.S.
- Increased competition
- National financial burdens

Strengths

Broad Product Portfolio

The company's product offerings consist of apparel, footwear and accessories for men, women and youth. For men and women, the company offers shirts and tops such as short sleeves, sleeveless and tanks, graphic t-shirts, long sleeves, and hoodies and sweatshirts; underwear; warm-ups and jackets; and bottoms such as shorts, pants, leggings and tights. The company also offers outerwear for men and sports bras for women. For kids, the company offers shirts, tops and bottoms for boys and girls. The footwear product line includes footwear related to sports such as football, baseball, lacrosse and soccer cleats, and slides. Under Armour also offers performance training footwear, running footwear, basketball footwear and hunting boots. The accessories product line consists of backpacks and bags, headwear, gloves, socks, sunglasses, equipment, protective gear, and mouth guards for men, women, and kids. At the end of FY2014, the company generated 76.4% of its revenues from apparel category, 14.4% from footwear category, and 9.2% from accessories category. Broad product offering proves to be the company's strength as it aids Under Armour in catering to different markets and minimizes risks of being dependent on single segment for revenues.

Strong Financial Performance

Under Armour has recorded strong financial performance in the past few years. The company's revenues increased at a compound annual growth rate (CAGR) of 30% from $1,063.9 million in FY2010 to $3,084.4 million in FY2014. The increase in revenues has been driven by the growing consumer interest in performance products as well as strong recognition of the Under Armour brand in the market. Its revenues grew by 32.3% in FY2014 compared to FY2013. This was mainly due to strong growth in direct to consumer sales in North America, driven by increase in square footage in the company's factory house stores, and continued growth in e-commerce business. The revenue growth was also attributable to increase in net sales in other foreign countries, primarily due to increased distribution and unit volume growth in the company's EMEA and Latin America operating segments; and unit growth driven by increased distribution and new offerings in multiple product categories, including continued growth of training, outdoor and golf apparel product lines, along with growth in footwear due to a broader assortment of running and basketball shoes, including new UA SpeedForm footwear.

In addition, the operating income and the net income of the company grew at a CAGR of 33% and 32%, respectively, between FY2010 and FY2014. The operating income and net income grew by 33.5% and 28.2%, respectively, in FY2014 over FY2013. Strong financial performance will provide the company with financial flexibility and also help in expansion activities.

Strong Marketing Presence

The company has embarked on a highly competitive marketing campaign. Taking cues from competitors such as Nike and Adidas, Under Armor Armour is maintaining a high presence in public eye. Through celebrity endorsements, public blitz, and a prominent, visible marketing campaign.

Strong Brand Loyalty

Under Armour benefits from a strong brand loyalty. Under Armour is regarded as a highly respected organization. Consumers who purchase from Under Armour are often satisfied and likely to be repeat customers. Loyal customers tend to buy exclusively from Under Armour stores.

Weaknesses

Dependence on Third-Party Suppliers and Manufacturers

Under Armour depends on third-party suppliers and manufacturers outside the US to provide fabrics and to produce its products, and therefore, has little control over the quality of products. In FY2014, approximately 65% of the fabric used in the company's products was sourced from five suppliers located in Taiwan, Singapore, Mexico and El Salvador. In addition, majority of the company's products are manufactured by unaffiliated manufacturers, and in FY2014, nearly 52% of its products were produced by 10 manufacturers. In FY2014, the products of Under Armour were manufactured by 29 primary manufacturers, operating in 14 countries, with approximately 65% of products manufactured in China, Jordan, Vietnam and Indonesia. The company has no long-term contracts with its suppliers or manufacturing sources. Therefore, any failure on the part of manufacturers to achieve and maintain high manufacturing standards could lead to manufacturing errors resulting in product recalls or withdrawals, delays or interruptions in production, cost overruns or other problems that could seriously harm the company's business. The company's reliance on third-party suppliers makes it difficult to ensure the quality of the goods sold in its outlets, and may lead to product recalls. This, in turn, could have an adverse effect on customer retention and brand loyalty.

Weak Presences Outside of the US

Under Armour has yet to establish itself as a prominent, global entity. Around 90% of its revenues originate in the United States. Under Armour has yet to focus its initiatives on gaining exposure in the international markets.

Opportunities

Innovation

The e-commerce sales have been growing at a fast pace in recent times as the online channel is growing in popularity as the most preferred channel for several customers. According to the US Department of Commerce, online retail sales in the US increased in 2013.Total retail sales, on the other hand, grew by only 4.3% during 2013. In this E-commerce sales accounted for 5.8% of total retail sales in 2013. This is not only happening in the United States a similar trend is noticed in Europe. According to industry estimates, the online retail sales in Europe grew by more than 18% in 2014 as compared to 2013. In addition, the online retail market in Asia and the Middle East and Africa are also witnessing growth. Under Armour offers all of its products online at www.underarmour.com. By leveraging its offerings online, the company can tap into a customer base which is increasingly using the web in search of better deals.

Positive Outlook for the Athletic Footwear Market in the US

The athletic footwear market in the US registered an increase in sales in the recent past. Under Armour sells athletic footwear for men, women and youth. Its product offering includes football shoes, baseball shoes, lacrosse shoes, softball and soccer cleats, slides, performance training footwear, running footwear, basketball footwear and hunting boots. With the athletic footwear market in the US growing, Under Armour is well positioned to generate revenues from this category. That's a good thing, though, since it means that the company has a huge opportunity in this competitive sector. And we expect big strides to be made in the years which should help Under Armour gain ground in key international geographies and underpenetrated sports realms.

Consumer Outlet

The company has opened more factory outlet shops that let the company clear its inventory. This not only helps clear the inventory, but it allows them to reach out to rural and suburban U.S. markets. The company will continue to open outlet shops not only in the United States, but also in Europe and Latin America. This will help Under Armour to better manage its inventory, and it should also help to build greater brand awareness.

Increasing Awareness

The company expanded its global presence by designing the outfits of several U.S. teams at the 2014 Winter Olympics in Sochi. As a result of this venture Under Armour managed to grab an eight-year extension of its deal with the U.S. Speed skating team. The deal extends all the way through to the 2022 Olympics. The company will also issue outfits to the U.S. gymnastics teams at the 2016 Summer Olympics in Rio de Janeiro and the 2020 Games in Tokyo.

In Latin America, Under Armour has also targeted Mexico, Chile, and Brazil, which hosted the 2014 World Cup and will host the 2016 Summer Olympics. In January the company's direct to consumer business became operational in Mexico and it will do the same in Brazil and Chile later in the year. In Chile, it also signed a deal to become the official outfit sponsor of Chilean soccer giant, Colo Colo. Late last year, Under Armour opened a brand new high concept store, called the "Experience Store", in Shanghai, China. Under Armour sells its products directly to consumers through its 13 stores in China, with the store count expected to grow by the end of this year.

International Expansion

Under Armour is growing at a high pace and is always looking for new ways to gain growth in the sports market. The overseas market is estimated at 130 billion so it is important for the company to have its presence known. Under Armour has established a group of international leaders to take care of sales and distribution in select countries. These efforts should about $1 billion or so to revenues.

Broaden the Target Market

With the majority of sporting goods sales to men, industry participants are always looking to widen their demographic reach to include more women and children. Under Armour has made a lot of changes to reach the women's apparel segment, improving the quality and styles of its collections and signing up high-profile endorsers like model Gisele Bundchen. The company is not only targeting women but also children, increasing its inventories to include more women and children's apparel. These initiatives should further enhance the company's growth profile over time.

Threats

Low barriers to entry

Companies in the sporting goods retail industry are exposed to tough competition as the industry has low barriers to entry primarily due to low capital investment. Low capital investment makes it rather easy for new players to enter the industry thereby increasing competition and pressurizing profit margins. Additionally, in the sporting goods retail industry, the suppliers hold a significant amount of power. As a result, suppliers can easily integrate forward and cap the existing companies' market share. However, backward integration for the retailers is comparatively tough, as it requires development of competencies in areas of manufacturing, designing products, distribution, branding, and after-sale servicing. Developing these competencies would demand additional financial investment. These factors, among others, tend to discourage retailers from integrating backwards. Thus, low barriers to entry subject Under Armour to intense competition and may limit its market share growth.

Rising Labor Wages in the U.S.

Labor costs have been rising in the US. The federal minimum wage rate in the US, which remained at $5.15 per hour since 1998, increased to $5.85 per hour in 2008. It further increased to $6.55 per hour in 2009 and to $7.25 per hour in 2010. Moreover, many states and municipalities in the country have minimum wage rate even higher than $7.25 per hour due to higher cost of living. The minimum wage rate has increased in the states of Arizona (from $7.8 in 2013 to $7.9 in 2014), Colorado (from $7.78 in 2013 to $8 in 2014), Florida (from $7.79 in 2013 to $7.93 in 2014), Ohio (from $7.85 in 2013 to $7.95 in 2014), Oregon (from $8.95 in 2013 to $9.1 in 2014) and Washington (from $9.19 in 2013 to $9.32 in 2014) in the recent past. The increase in labor costs in its key market will affect the company's margins.

Competition

There are always risks when you take on an industry leader. NIKE could increase competition because of the power that it has in the market. Nike has around 6 billion in assets so they could outbid the company for endorsement deals and secure cheaper sourcing plants in emerging markets. Under Armour will need to stay creative in their approach.

Financial Burdens

Increasing taxes and interest rates hurt the company economically. The company would have to increase the price of its products in order to make a profit. Raising prices will hurt their profits because of increased competition from substitutable products.

TOWS MATRIX	STRENGTHS – S 1. Broad product portfolios 2. Strong financial performance 3. Strong marketing presence 4. Strong brand loyalty	WEAKNESSES – W 1. Dependence on third party suppliers 2. Weak presence outside US
OPPORTUNITIES – O 1. Positive outlook for athletic footwear market in US 2. Consumer outlet 3. Increasing awareness 4. International expansions 5. Broaden the target market	SO STRATEGIES 1. Embark on a strong marketing program in foreign territories. 2. Continue utilizing marketing campaigns to increase awareness in the global market. 3. Create a marketing strategy that introduces the brand to new consumers. 4. Sponsor different types of marathons to boost footwear sales.	WO STRATEGIES 1. Focus on increasing awareness in foreign territories. 2. Develop focus groups for foreign territories to account for differences in taste and consumer preference.
THREATS – T 1. Low barriers to entry 2. Rising labor wages in the US 3. Competition 4. Financial burden	ST STRATEGIES 1. Use social media to access and talk with current and potential customers to gain competitive advantage. 2. Focus on hiring and training independent and autonomous workers to cut back on payroll. Hire on attitude – not skills.	WT STRATEGIES 1. Focus on beating competition to gain dependence on third party suppliers.

J. Market Share Data Graph

Athletic & Sporting Good Manufacturing Market Share

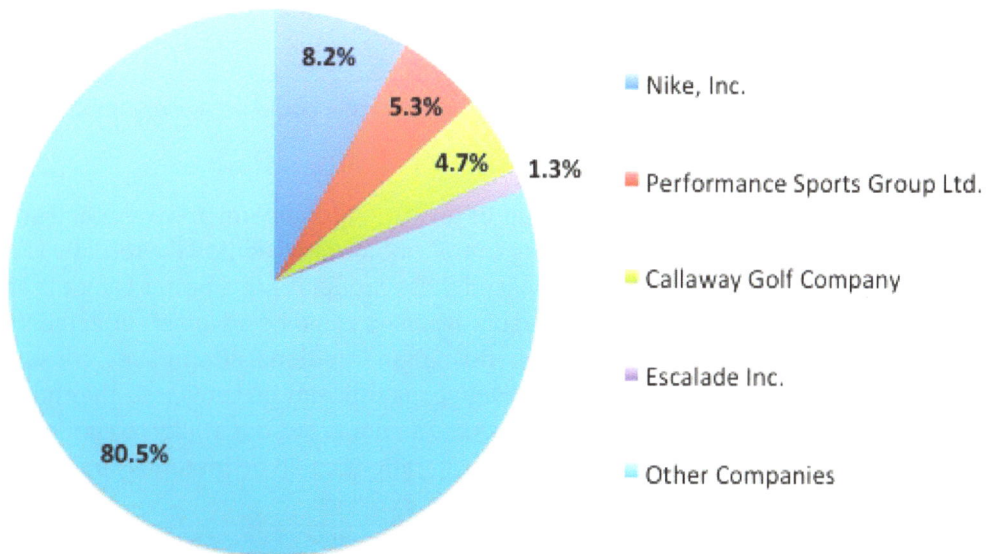

Company	Market Share
Nike, Inc.	8.2%
Performance Sports Group Ltd.	5.3%
Callaway Golf Company	4.7%
Escalade Inc.	1.3%
Other	80.5%

As evidence by the graph above, Under Armour does not hold a considerable market share in the Athletic & Sporting Good Manufacturing Industry--Nike and Performance Sports Group are the key players and hold an 8.2% and 5.3% share respectively. Even when Under Armour is compared to it's rivals in the Textile/Apparel Industry, it still does not hold a considerable share.

II. <u>FOCAL POINTS FOR ACTION</u>

Identification of problems and issues that need to be resolved.
Analyzation of risk factors from 10K.

A. <u>Short Range</u> (Source: SEC, 2014)

Sales of performance products may not continue to grow and this could adversely impact our ability to grow our business.

We believe continued growth in industry-wide sales of performance apparel, footwear and accessories will be largely dependent on consumers continuing to transition from traditional alternatives to performance products. If consumers are not convinced these products are a better choice than traditional alternatives, growth in the industry and our business could be adversely affected. In addition, because performance products are often more expensive than traditional alternatives, consumers who are convinced these products provide a better alternative may still not be convinced they are worth the extra cost. If industry-wide sales of performance products do not grow, our ability to continue to grow our business and our financial condition and results of operations could be materially adversely impacted.

Our profitability may decline as a result of increasing pressure on pricing.

Our industry is subject to significant pricing pressure caused by many factors, including intense competition, consolidation in the retail industry, pressure from retailers to reduce the costs of products and changes in consumer demand. These factors may cause us to reduce our prices to retailers and consumers, which could negatively impact our margins and cause our profitability to decline if we are unable to offset price reductions with comparable reductions in our operating costs. This could have a material adverse effect on our results of operations and financial conditions.

B. <u>Long Range</u> (Source: SEC, 2014)

We must continue to effectively manage our growth and the increased complexity of a global business or we may not achieve our long-term growth targets and our brand image, net revenues and profitability may decline.

We have expanded our business and operations rapidly since our inception and our net revenues have increased to $3,963.3 million in 2015 from $1,472.7 million in 2011. Our long-term growth strategy depends on our ability to not only maintain strong growth throughout our business, but to also successfully execute on strategic growth initiatives in key areas, such as our international business, footwear and our global direct to consumer sales channel. Our growth in these areas depends on our ability to continue to successfully expand our global network of brand and factory house stores, grow our e-commerce and mobile application offerings throughout the world and continue to successfully increase our product offerings and market share in footwear. If we cannot effectively execute our long-term growth strategies, our business and results of operations could be negatively impacted.

In addition to successfully executing on our long-term growth strategies, we must also continue to successfully manage the operational difficulties associated with expanding our business to meet increased consumer demand throughout the world. We may experience difficulties in obtaining sufficient raw materials and manufacturing capacity to produce our products, as well as delays in production and shipments, as our products are subject to risks associated with overseas sourcing and manufacturing. We must also continually evaluate the need to expand critical functions in our business, including sales and marketing, product development and distribution functions, our management information systems and other processes and technology. To support these functions, we must hire, train and manage an increasing number of employees, and obtain more space to support our expanding workforce. We may not be successful in undertaking these types of initiatives cost effectively or at all, and could experience serious operating difficulties if we fail to do so. These growth efforts could also increase the strain on our existing resources. If we experience difficulties in supporting the growth of our business, we could experience an erosion of our brand image and a decrease in net revenues and net income.

If we fail to successfully manage or realize expected results from acquisitions and other significant investments, it may have a material adverse effect on our results of operations and financial position, as well as negatively impact the price of our publicly traded common stock.

From time to time we may engage in acquisition opportunities we believe are complementary to our business and brand. For example, as part of our ongoing business strategy we have engaged in acquisitions to grow and enhance our Connected Fitness business. In order to successfully execute this strategy, we must manage the integration of acquired companies and employees successfully. Because our Connected Fitness business is a relatively new line of business for us, these challenges may be more pronounced. Integrating acquisitions can also require significant efforts and resources, which could divert management attention from more profitable business operations.

Failing to successfully integrate acquired entities and businesses or to produce results consistent with financial models used in the analysis of our acquisitions could potentially result in an impairment of goodwill and intangible assets, which could have a material adverse effect on our results of operations and financial position. In addition, we may not be successful in our efforts to continue to grow the number of users, maintain or increase user engagement or ultimately realize expected revenues from our Connected Fitness community. For example, we may not successfully increase sales of our apparel, footwear and accessory products to these users. Any of these developments could have a material adverse effect on our results of operations and financial position, as well as negatively impact the price of our publicly traded common stock.

III. DEVELOP ALTERNATIVES
Equate to strategy types corporate/business.

A. Consider Generic Industry Type & Industry Characteristics

Alternative Strategy #1: Best Cost Provider Strategy in international markets.

Nike and Adidas are well established in foreign markets such as China. Under Armour sales/revenue is predominantly from North America. Therefore, to be competitive in China, they must employ this hybrid strategy that balance strategic emphasis on a lower cost and differentiation. This strategy will allow UA to aim squarely at value-conscious buyers in China who are looking for a better product.

Pros
- UA proven effective track record of upscale attributes in it product offering
- China has the second largest economy in the world

Cons
- The industry leader, Nike is well established in China and are able to offer a lower price to continue to siphon customer away from UA
- Regulations in China are vastly different than the U.S.

Alternative Strategy #2: Merger

With over 90% of its revenues being earned in the North America, Under Armour will benefit by merging with a corporation that has established international success. Therefore, a viable strategy is to merge with Nike. The greatest advantage for Under Armour is a deal that will allow it to be a separate entity and retain its name and direction. This will ultimately permit access to more NBA and NFL licenses. Altogether, this will be a win-win for both, as Nike will have access to Under Armour moisture wicking technology.

Pros
- Access to teams and athletes that Nike provide apparel for domestically and internationally
- Synergy against the Adidas-Reebok combination (2005 merger)
- Extra tools to meet and exceed expectations
- Less to worry about financially
- Footwear line

Cons
- The possibility of the lack of synergy
- Under Armour could lose its name and dissolve
- Possible redundancy

B. Boston Consulting Group Matrix (Build/hold/harvest/divest)

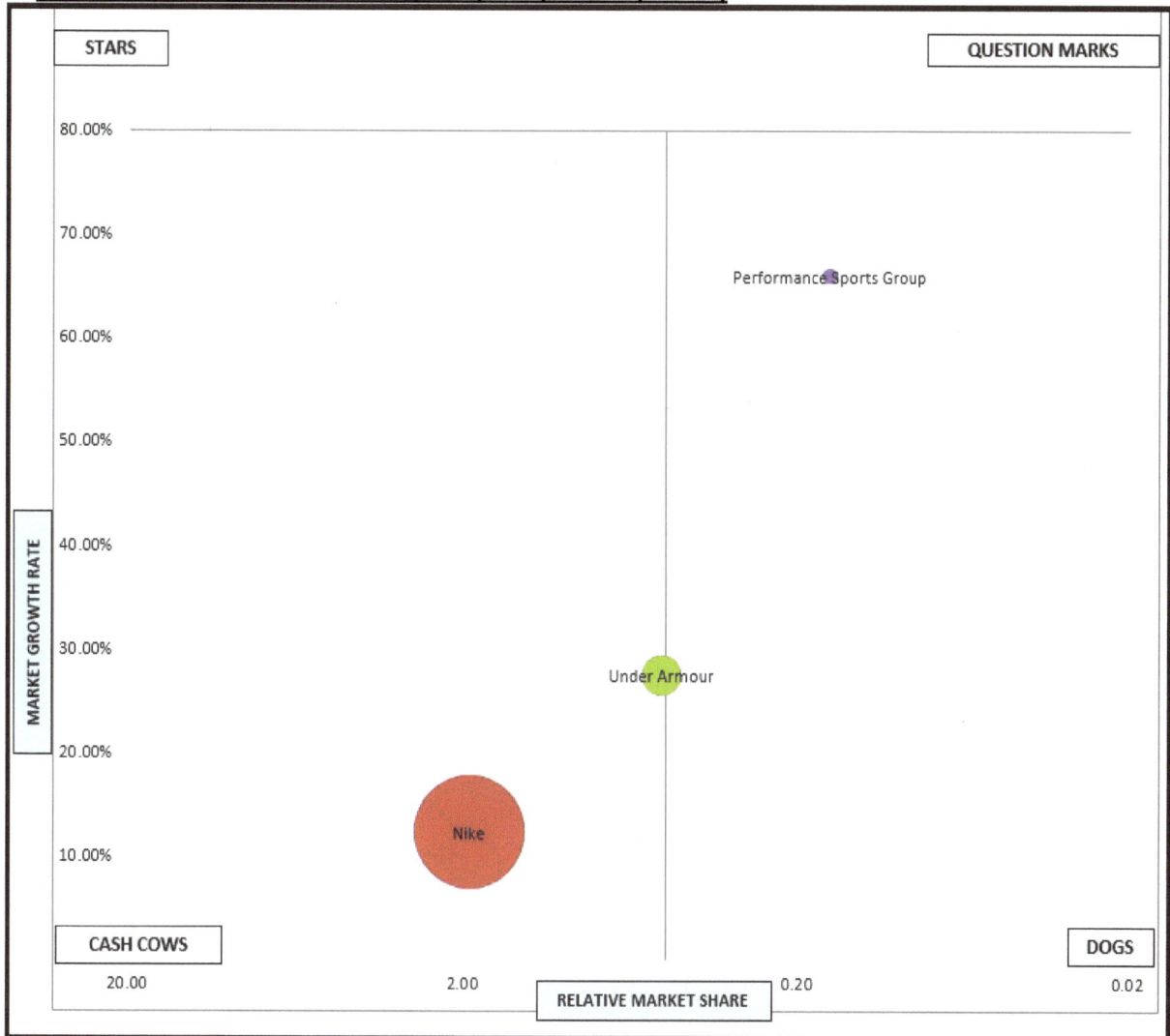

Under Armour is considered a Cash Cow because of its abilities to generate Cash. They have the second highest market share next to Nike and they are considered to be a Market challenger. Their products have been able to generate steady streams of cash flows helping fuel the company.

C. Competitive Position (Leader/Challenger/Follower/Nicher)

When CEO Plank created the compressed clothing the company entered a niche market. Everything Under Armour sold was specialized at first they just specialized for Football Players and Baseball players. Now they have expanded the line to include all types of sports. Under Armour recently became the second largest sportswear company in the U.S. by total sales thanks to impressive total U.S. sales growth in both its growing apparel line and footwear segment. The company will continue to focus on creating innovative and high-quality products, breaking into new segments, and continuing to keep a niche-market image.

D. Competitive Strategy Options (Overall low cost leadership/differentiation/focus)

Under Armour incorporates a broad differentiation strategy. They have been able to produce a competitive edge by incorporating attributes and features that set their products offering apart from rivals in ways that buyers consider a higher quality, valuable and worth paying for. Under Armour's strategy is based on brand identity and technological advance product performance. Their success has allowed them to command a premium price for its apparel as well as gain buyer loyalty. Additionally, Under Armour experienced first mover advantage in performance sports apparel which has been giving marketing exposure through high-performing athletes on the high school, collegiate, and professional level.

E. Appraise Each Alternative/Overall Organization Impact (Rumelt's Criteria)

In order to evaluate Under Armour's business strategy, Rumelt's criteria will help to organize and analyze business strategies to assess their alignment with organizational interests as well as gauge their effectiveness and efficiency.

Rumelt's Criteria - Under Armour

Strategy	Consistency	Consonance	Feasibility	Advantage	Total
Market Penetration					
▫ Pricing Strategies	2	2	3	2	9
▫ Focus on marketing footwear products	2	2	4	4	12
▫ Increase Global Marketing Presence	2	3	4	5	14
Market Development					
▫ Global Expansion Europe, Asia	4	3	4	5	16
▫ Expand distribution services to new foreign territories	3	3	3	4	13
▫ Develop exclusive corporate sponsor and supplier contracts	2	2	3	3	10
▫ Develop exclusive partnerships with universities to be official outfitter	3	3	3	4	13
Product Development					
▫ Footwear Products	3	3	4	5	15
▫ Develop "fit band" technology	4	4	5	5	18
Concentric Diversification					
▫ Diversify product line to football cleat market	3	3	3	3	12
▫ Acquire "My Fitness"	3	3	4	5	15
▫ Develop healthy food products(Water, Energy Bar, Energy Drinks)	2	2	2	3	10
Horizontal Integration					

▢ Increased operations in footwear products	3	3	4	5	15
▢ Acquire Nike Inc. or other competitors	3	3	2	4	12
Backward Vertical Integration					
▢ Control over distribution centers to increase customer satisfaction	3	3	2	3	11
▢ Acquire materials supplier	1	2	1	2	6
Forward Vertical Integration					
▢ Partner with Bolster to expand distribution centers globally	2	2	2	1	7
▢ Open more retail stores	2	2	2	3	9
▢ Redesign online store	2	1	1	1	5
Conglomerate Diversification					
▢ Purchase technology firm	2	2	2	2	8
▢ Purchase legal firm	1	2	2	2	7
Divestiture					
▢ Sale of company stock	3	4	4	2	13
▢ Divest Focus Point HQ	2	2	4	4	12

IV. DECISION AND RECOMMENDATION

Choose the best strategic alternative for each level:

A.) Corporate

ANSOFF MATRIX	PRODUCTS Present	PRODUCTS New
MARKETS Present	**Market Penetration** ☐ Offers an increasing range of styles and colors in its original apparel lines by 2016	**Product Development** ☐ Company growth by offering modified or new products to current market segments.
MARKETS New	**Market Extension** ☐ Global Expansion	**Diversification** ☐ Introducing a family of new devices for tracking sleep, fitness, and nutrition.

☐ **Objective:** Market Penetration: Offers an increasing range of styles and colors in its original apparel lines by 2016
- ☐ **Strategies**
  - ☐ Implementation of wide range of products in different styles by 2016
  - ☐ Implementation of wide range of products in new colors for summer of 2016
  - ☐ Continue with wide range of products for all ages

☐ **Objective:** Product Development: Company growth by offering modified or new products to current market segments.
- ☐ **Strategies**
  - ☐ Modify existing products
  - ☐ Continue new product development to present markets

☐ **Objective:** Market Extension through global expansion: increase foreign market sales to at least 10% of total revenues by 2015.
- ☐ **Strategies**
  - ☐ Making available current products to new markets
  - ☐ Focus on infrastructure being built outside North America
  - ☐ Focusing on partnering with international manufacturers and distributors and building own Under Armour Stores abroad

☐ **Objective:** Diversification: Introducing a family of new devices for tracking sleep, fitness, and nutrition.
- ☐ **Strategies**
  - ☐ Introduction of the MapMyFitness App
  - ☐ Partnership with HTC phone company to create the healthbox
  - ☐ Acquiring Endomondo App

B.) Business

- **Objective:** Increase gross profits by 60% (from $1.13 billion to $1.81) by 2016.
  - **Strategies**
    - Build brand equity, customers' perception of Under Armour's image, brand loyalty, and trust with customers in order to raise prices
      - Acquiring new partnerships/licenses with organizations and sponsoring ships of key athletes to build relationships, strengthen connections, and increase visibility of brand.
      - Focus on innovation of new and existing products

C.) Functional

- **Objective:** Align and educate entire company regarding emerging athlete-focused, holiday marketing strategy by mid 2014 and implement marketing campaign over the following year.
  - Strategies
    - Create a holiday-type, hard-hitting marketing campaigns as opposed to trickling brand throughout market in order to contain marketing costs and maintain 11% (operational costs) marketing budget
    - Human Resources: reinforce through onboarding and current employee education regarding company mission/vision/values/wills

V. <u>IMPLEMENTATION</u> (Goals/Participants/Steps)

A.) <u>Corporate</u>

Based on Rumelt's criteria, it has been identified that global expansion is a strategy that is the most consistent, consonant, feasible, and an advantage for the company to pursue.

- **Objective:** Increase foreign market sales to at least 10% of total revenues by 2015.
  - **Strategy:** Global expansion will be achieved by making available current products to new markets, focusing on infrastructure being built outside North America, focusing on partnering with international manufacturers and distributors, and building our own Under Armour Stores abroad.
    - **Who will implement strategy?**
      - Chief Executive Officer, Kevin A. Plank
      - Chief Revenue Officer, & International President, Karl-Heinz (Charlie) Maurath
      - Lead Director, A.B Krongard
      - Chief Financial Officer, Lawrence (Chip) Molloy
      - Executive Vice President, Global Operations, James H Hardy Jr
      - Executive Vice President, Global Marketing, Matthew C. Mirchin
    - **How will the strategy achieve organization wide commitment?**
      - The strategy will achieve organization wide commitment because it provides opportunities for each organization member, as well as for the organization itself, to develop to their full potential. The strategy also create an environment in which it is possible to find exciting and challenging work
    - **Are structuring mechanism properly aligned?**
      - Structuring mechanism are properly aligned. There is a value proposition which give the project value which lead into the profit proposition. This brings in money for the company then the people proposition which gives the workers motivation to execute the project.
    - **Does leadership inspire commitment to strategy?**
      - Leadership does inspire commitment to strategy they want the amount of sales to be a good portion of total revenue in the year 2015. They motivate their employees across the globe to sell more. They incentivize their employees in order to reach their desired goals.
    - **Do reward systems reinforce appropriate behavior?**
      - Reward systems do reinforce appropriate behavior. Without the reward systems sales personnel would just be encouraged to sell the bare minimum. Even if the bare minimum reaches the company goals it is always better to strive for more.
    - **Are functional issues addressed and resolved in implementation?**
      - Yes functional issues are resolved in the implementation. One functional issue that we have is how do we make our company more market and customer driven. We analyzed this and figured that we use our sales model and track every aspect of it. We also collect reports and ample input from customers and prospects.
    - **Is the strategy communicated properly?**

⸬ The strategy is communicated properly to all of our customers. Not just through our advertisements but through the countless employees and through the products we sell. We strive on producing and giving a service to our customers so that they could feel comfortable in our products. They could purchase a product that they like and is available in different shapes and sizes. A product that will be able to withstand the obstacles that you put it threw. Our customers will see that our products are superior to our competitors and will demand our products. This will thus raise our profits and raise our foreign market revenues.

B.) Business

⸬ **Objective:** Increase gross profits by 60% (from $1.13 billion to $1.81) by 2016.

⸬ **Strategy:** Build brand equity, customers' perception of Under Armour's image, brand loyalty, and trust with customers in order to raise prices by acquiring new partnerships/licenses with organizations and sponsoring ships of key athletes to build relationships, strengthen connections, and increase visibility of brand, and focusing on innovation of new and existing products.

⸬ **Who will implement strategy?**
  - ⸬ Chief Executive Officer, Kevin A. Plank
  - ⸬ Chief Financial Officer, Lawrence (Chip) Molloy
  - ⸬ Chief Revenue Officer, Karl-Heinz (Charlie) Maurath
  - ⸬ Chief Operating Officer, Brad Dickerson
  - ⸬ Chief Merchandising Officer, Henry B. Stafford
  - ⸬ Executive Vice President Global Operations, James H Hardy Jr.
  - ⸬ Chief Digital Officer, Robin Thurston
  - ⸬ Senior Vice President of Sales, Adam Peake
    - ⸬ All sales and clientele relations teams (all levels from management to staff)

⸬ **How will the strategy achieve organization wide commitment?**
  - ⸬ The customer experience with our product is dependent on the quality of the product and the service that the consumer receives by the sales personnel.
    - ⸬ Current sales and clientele relations teams will be incentivized to not only gain more sponsorships, customers, and contracts, but maintain the current ones with the best customer service possible in the industry.
      - ⸬ Financial rewards (apart from yearly cost of living raises) would help to facilitate high performance. Scorecards will monitor for increased customer satisfaction, increase of number of new customers/contracts.
      - ⸬ The strategy achieves an organization wide commitment because of the benefits that come with it.
    - ⸬ In regard to development of new products, the research and development team will be informed of the strategy and intent to continue the organization's dedication to innovation.

⸬ **Are structuring mechanism properly aligned?**

- Structuring mechanisms are properly aligned--all appropriate parties within the organization are involved, informed, and aligned with the strategic goal at hand.
- We have a value proposition of the benefits and value that the organization can deliver to its customers by its products.
- Next we have a profit proposition that enables to make a profit out of the value proposition.

- **Are functional area conflicts reconciled to strategy requirements?**
    - There were a couple sources of conflict that were reconciled because of the implementation of the strategy. There was a communication problem between management and workers. That was stemmed primarily because of workers. The management team assessed the situation and acknowledged the fact that certain workers did more than others. The implementation of financial incentives through monitoring of a scorecard helped to rectify the situation. Leadership inspires commitment to strategy because they believe that with increased workers performance this will increase the output of products further increasing profits.

- **Do reward systems reinforce appropriate behavior?**
    - Reward systems due in fact reinforce appropriate behavior because workers see that their coworkers are getting awarded for doing what is right and increasing productivity. Employees see that their coworkers are receiving increased wages and they want the same treatment so they increase their productivity.
    - The financial incentive rewards a well-rounded employee as well as it is not about the number of sales/contracts, but the maintenance, retention, and satisfaction of that customer. If the client is satisfied this could lead to more referrals, which benefits the employee and company alike.

- **Are functional issues addressed and resolved in implementation?**
    - Financial incentives (including bonuses/commissions along with minimums/maximums) are made available to employees and management alike.
    - Communication of the strategic plan and how it affects every level (macro to meso to micro) is clearly and continually reiterated through review of scorecards and performance meetings.
    - If other issues arise during implementation, it is imperative that the plan be addressed and resolved in order to achieve the maximum effectiveness in reaching the objective. Any and all issues should be reported to your direct report.

- **Is the strategy communicated properly?**
    - The strategy is communicated properly we need to determine regular review cycles for all phases of the strategy. Ideally, the strategy should be reviewed once every quarter for executives assessing all elements of the strategy and its outcomes. Modification of the plan may be necessary, according to the revisions.
    - For meso level management, monitoring individuals' performance based on the metrics stated, should occur on a weekly basis along with

a monthly basis that would translate into (if applicable) the financial incentive.

C.) Functional

- **Objective:** Align and educate entire company regarding emerging athlete-focused, holiday marketing strategy by mid 2014 and implement marketing campaign over the following year.
  - **Strategy:** We will create a holiday-type, hard-hitting marketing campaigns as opposed to trickling brand throughout market in order to contain marketing costs and maintain 11% (operational costs) marketing budget. Human Resources will reinforce through onboarding and current employee education regarding company mission/vision/values/wills that this campaign is based upon.
    - **Who will implement strategy?**
      - Chief Executive Officer, Kevin A. Plank
      - Executive Vice President Global Marketing, Matthew Mirchin
      - Chief Digital Officer, Robin Thurston
      - Chief Merchandising Officer, Henry B. Stafford
      - Chief Human Resources Officer, Kerry D. Chandler
      - President, Footwear and Innovation, Kip J Fulks
      - President, International, Karl-Heinz Marauth
      - Executive Vice President, Global Operations James H Hardy Jr.
    - **How will the strategy achieve organization wide commitment?**
      - Human Resources plays an integral part in achieving a unified message that is portrayed to its targeted market. Not only does the department reinforce its key mission/vision/values/wills to new employees, but also it reinforces it to existing employees to gain buy in and employee loyalty to the brand. This assures that every employee lives the campaign through education of the company even if not directly involved in the marketing process.
      - The strategy will be perceived well by the organization, as the new marketing tactics will bring attention to the company to new and existing customers alike. It will hopefully bring in more endorsements by athletes who will want to represent the company (that simultaneously helps the business objective previously mentioned). This will drive in profits and in the long run increase revenues and while containing costs.
    - **Are structuring mechanism properly aligned?**
      - The project is in the planning stages: structuring mechanisms are properly aligned--all appropriate parties within the organization are involved, informed, and aligned with the strategic goal at hand.
      - We have a value proposition of the benefits and value that the organization can deliver to its customers through this strategy.
      - Costs have been calculated for the Human Resources education portion and marketing (remaining at 11%).
    - **Are functional area conflicts reconciled to strategy requirements?**
      - Functional area conflicts are not reconciled to strategy requirements.
    - **Does leadership inspire commitment to strategy?**
      - Leadership does inspire commitment to strategy. This inspiration helps with staff engagement. Leadership establishes a clear vision and are

able to paint this vision in the minds of the workers. They are effective in their communication and willing to spend more time communicating. They want change to happen. They are perceived as effective role models within the organization.

- **Do reward systems reinforce appropriate behavior?**
  - Reward systems do enforce appropriate behavior. The entire team was educated about new and emerging athlete focused holiday marketing strategy. If the team is able to boost profits through sales they will get a bonus. If they are unable to boost sales then there will be no bonus.
- **Are functional issues addressed and resolved in implementation?**
  - Functional issues are resolved in implementation. One problem that was solved was that the marketing team was spending too much time with the development team and did not have any time to support the sales team. In order for marketing to work there has to be sales generated. So we clearly defined the sales model outlining the activities and time required for each selling step. We also structured product planning as an ongoing process.
- **Is the strategy communicated properly?**
  - The strategy is communicated properly and it increases the company's chances to accurately transmit the product's benefits.

References

Windham, C. (n.d.) *How to Do a Rumelt Evaluation Method.* Retrieved from http://yourbusiness.azcentral.com/rumelt-evaluation-method-29008.html

CSIMarket. (2016). S*tocks, Under Armour, Inc.* Retrieved from http://csimarket.com/stocks/charts.php?code=UA

CSIMarket. (2014). *Under Armour (UA) Sales Per Country and Region.* Retrieved from http://csimarket.com/stocks/segments_geo.php?code=UA

GlobalData, Inc. (2016). B*usiness Description, Under Armour, Inc.* Retrieved from www.lexisnexis.com/hottopics/lnacademic

GlobalData, Inc. (2013). *Financial Ratios, Nike Inc.* Retrieved from www.lexisnexis.com/hottopics/lnacademic

GlobalData, Inc. (2016). *Financial Ratios, Under Armour, Inc.* Retrieved from www.lexisnexis.com/hottopics/lnacademic

Gurufocus. (2016). *Under Armour, Inc. (UA) Altman Z Score.* Retreived from http://www.gurufocus.com/term/zscore/UA/Altman-Z-Score/Under-Armour-Inc

Gurufocus. (2016). *Under Armour, Inc. (UA) Return on Equity.* Retreived from http://www.gurufocus.com/term/ROE/UA/Return-on-Equity/Under-Armour-Inc

Gurufocus. (2016). *Under Armour, Inc. (UA) Stock Analysis.* Retreived from http://www.gurufocus.com/stock/UA

IBISWorld. (2015). *IBISWorld Industry Report 33992a - Athletic & Sporting Goods Manufacturing in the US.* Retrieved from http://clients1.ibisworld.com.ezproxy.lewisu.edu/reports/us/industry/default.aspx?entid=895

Marcoaxis. (2016). *Under Armour Working Capital.* Retrieved from https://www.macroaxis.com/invest/ratio/UA--Working-Capital

New York Times. (2016). *Apparel & Accessories Industry Snapshot.* Retrieved from http://markets.on.nytimes.com/research/markets/usmarkets/industry.asp?industry=53222companies

Reuters. (2016). *Under Armour Inc. (UA) Company Profile.* Retrieved from http://www.reuters.com/finance/stocks/companyProfile?symbol=UA

Standard and Poor's. (2016). *Standard & Poor's Corporate Descriptions plus News.* Retrieved from www.lexisnexis.com/hottopics/lnacademic

Statista. (2016). *Under Armour - Statistics & Facts.* Retrieved from http://www.statista.com/topics/2470/under-armour/

Thompson, A., Peteraf, M., Gamble, J. & Strickland, A. J. (2016). Crafting & Executing Strategy. New York: McGraw Hill Education.

Statista. (2016). *U.S. Apparel Market - Statistics & Facts.* http://www.statista.com/topics/965/apparel-market-in-the-us/

Trefis. (2016). *Under Armour through the Lens of Porter's Five Forces.* Retrieved from http://www.trefis.com/stock/ua/articles/186040/under-armour-through-the-lens-of-porters-five-forces/2013-05-16

Trefis. (2016). *Nike Through the Lens of Porter's Five Forces.* Retrieved from http://www.trefis.com/stock/nke/articles/217421/marynike-through-the-lens-of-porters-five-forces/2013-12-02

Under Armour, Inc. (2015). *2014 Under Armour Annual Report.* Retrieved from http://files.shareholder.com/downloads/UARM/1635972756x0x816471/3BEBC664-8584-4F22-AC0B-844CB2949814/UA_2014_Annual_Report.PDF

Under Armour, Inc. (2014). *2013 Under Armour Annual report.* Retrieved from http://files.shareholder.com/downloads/UARM/1635972756x0x735952/1020FA20-6420-440E-8167-BCD7DB8D5422/2013_Annual_Report.pdf

Under Armour, Inc. (2016). *Investor Relations: Financials.* Retrieved from http://investor.underarmour.com/annuals.cfm

Under Armour, Inc. (2016). *Board of Directors.* Retrieved from http://investor.underarmour.com/directors.cfm

Under Armour, Inc. (2016). *Code of Conduct 2016.* Retrieved from http://files.shareholder.com/downloads/UARM/1635972756x0x873823/38F030C7-5348-4CC6-B8CD-81D68B2F496C/Code_of_Conduct_2016.pdf

Under Armour, Inc. (2016). *Code of Conduct for Suppliers.* Retrieved from http://www.uabiz.com/company/corpResponsibility.cfm

Under Armour, Inc. (2015). *Under Armour, Inc. Marketline Company Profile.* 1-29.

Under Armour, Inc. SWOT Analysis." Under Armour, Inc. SWOT Analysis (2014): 1-7. Business Source Complete.

Under Armour, Inc. (2016). *Investor Relations: Financials.* Retrieved from http://investor.underarmour.com/annuals.cfm

U.S. Securities and Exchange Commission (SEC). (2014). *Under Armor, Inc. Annual Report on Form 10-K.* Retrieved from http://www.sec.gov/Archives/edgar/data/1336917/000133691715000006/ua-20141231x10k.htm

Yahoo! Finance. (2016) *UA Income Statement.* Retrieved from https://finance.yahoo.com/q/is?s=UA+Income+Statement&annual

Yahoo! Finance. (2016). *UA Industry: Textile - Apparel Clothing.* Retrieved from https://finance.yahoo.com/q/in?s=UA+Industry

Yahoo! Finance. (2016). *UA Balance Sheet.* Retrieved from https://finance.yahoo.com/q/bs?s=UA+Balance+Sheet&annual

YCharts. (2016). *Under Armour Tobin's Q (Approximate) (Quarterly) (UA).* Retrieved from https://ycharts.com/companies/UA/tobin_q

Zacks. (2016). *Under Armour-a: (UA) Comparison to Industry.* Retrieved from http://www.zacks.com/stock/research/UA/industry-comparison

www.ingramcontent.com/pod-product-compliance
Lightning Source LLC
Chambersburg PA
CBHW052053190326
41519CB00002BA/204